Rivāyat-i Hēmīt-i Ašawahistān

Edition, Transcription
and
Translation

A Study in Zoroastrian Law

by
Nezhat Safa-Isfehani

Harvard Iranian Series

Volume Two

Richard N. Frye
Editor

SBN 0-674-77305-5

Library of Congress Catalog Card Number

Printed by the Harvard University Printing Office

Foreword

SINCE the first volume of the Harvard Iranian series appeared much time has passed and costs and problems of printing have increased. In the past, printers could set Greek, Arabic and other Oriental texts whereas today it has become almost prohibitive to print an English text, not to mention other languages, especially esoteric Middle Persian texts. Therefore in the future we will seek to publish scholarly volumes by photography of typed manuscripts, which is the case with the present work. It was originally decided to reproduce those folios of the text found in the manuscript TD2, originally in the possession of B. Anklesaria and now housed in the library of the K.R. Cama Oriental Institute in Bombay. This has now appeared as volume 54 of the Pahlavi Text series of Shiraz University, making a duplication of the task unnecessary, and the reader is referred to that facsimile of the manuscript if desired. Ms. Safa-Isfehani's work is based on B. Anklesaria's edition of the same manuscript.

The present complete English translation of this text which has been presented by Ms. Safa-Isfehani in partial fulfillment of the requirements for the degree of Doctor of Philosophy, Columbia University, will be of aid to those who do not read Middle Persian and it will assist those students of Zoroastrianism and comparative religions who seek information about the legal and religious problems of Zoroastrians under Muslim rule.

English is not the native tongue of the translator, so the indulgence of the reader is requested for any infelicities of language. I have endeavored to correct errors in typing but have not otherwise touched the text or translation. A discussion about the text, the author and manuscripts may be found in the introduction to the edition by B.T. Anklesaria, published in Bombay in 1962.

The author has spent years on this text, in the difficult Middle Persian (Pahlavi) language, which presents problems of decipherment well known to Iranists but unsuspected by others. It is hoped that the present translation will aid the interested reader to better understand Zoroastrian and ancient Iranian jurisprudence.

Richard N. Frye

A Word From The Author

THE difficulties of reading and deciphering the Pahlavi language did not prevent me from dedicating years of endeavor to deciphering one of the most difficult Pahlavi legal texts.

The present work after being several times re-examined by myself, has been thoroughly read by Drs. Dale Bishop and Christopher Brunner of Columbia University. It has also been taken to Bombay for the inspection of Daṣtur Dr. Hormazdyār K. Mirza of Bombay University. Further it was carefully read by Dastur Firoze Kotwal, visiting scholar at the Center for the Study of World Religions, Harvard University.

My deepest gratitude goes to all these scholars who have so patiently and authoritatively examined my work. Nevertheless, should there be any flaw I alone am responsible. I would sincerely appreciate any criticism or any suggested different readings.

Nezhat Safa-Isfehani

TABLE OF CONTENTS

Abbreviations

ANK.	Anklesaria (B.T. Anklesaria)
Av.	Avesta
Bd.	Bundahišn
B.P.	Bahman Punjyā
BSOAS.	Bulletin of the School of Oriental and African Studies, London
BTE.	B. T. Anklesaria's edition of Rivāyat-i Hēmīt Ašawahištān
DB.	Dhabhar
Dd.	Dādestān-i Denīg
Dk.	Dēnkard
DK.M.	Dēnkard Madan
D. BZ.	Dastur Barzu
ES.	A. Christensen, L'Empire des Sassanids, (Kobenhaven, 1907)
FS.	Farnbag Srōš (his Rivāyat, ed. Anklesaria)
KB	Kama Bohra
K.J.	Kaikhusroo M. Jamasp Asa
KK.	Kaus Kama
Men.	Jean De Menasce
MK.	MacKenzie Pahlavi Dictionary
Mh.D.	Mādayān-i Hazār Dādestān
Mh.D.S.J.B.	The Laws of the Ancient Persians as Found in the Mātikān-i Hazār Dādestān, translated by S. J. Bulsara, (Fort Printing Publication, Bombay, 1937)
MS.	Manuscript TD2
NY.	Nyāyišn
NSL.	A. Bartholomae, "Notes on Sassanian Law," Cama Oriental Institute Publications, translation by L. Bogdanov, Bombay, 1931-67.
OPH.	H. K. Mirza, Outlines of Parsi History, Bombay, 1974
Pah.	Pahlavi
R.	Rivāyat
R.HF.	Persian Rivāyats of Hormazdyār Farāmarz, translated by Dhabhar (Bombay, 1932)
SBE	Sacred Books of the East, ed. F. Max Muller, Oxford, 1887.
Sd.Bd.	Saddar Bundihišn
ŠKW.	Škand-i gumānig wizar
Vd.	Vendidād
Y.	Yasna
Yt.	Yašt

INTRODUCTION

The present work is the first complete translation
of the Pahlavi text of the Rivāyat-i Hēmīt-i Ašwahistān,
"The Religious Explanation of Hēmīt, the son of Ašwahišt."
Dating from the late ninth or early tenth century, it is
a collection of religious, social, and civil laws based
on the Zoroastrian religious codes, and reflects faithfully
the Zoroastrian religious outlooks, creed and practice that
prevailed in Persia in the Sasanian era (from A.D.224 to
A.D. 640). The rules are either based on Avestan laws or
are adaptations from the Avesta (the Zoroastrian scriptures).
The purpose of these practical laws was to create an organized,
prosperous society that would be harmonious in all its relationships, as well as to guarantee the peace of the soul in
the next world and a blissful afterlife.

The concept of law was an essential part of
Zoroastrianism from its earliest stages. Even the earliest
[legendary] royal dynasty of Iranian peoples was Av. Paradāta,
later Pēšdād, "The Ancient Law-Giver." One-third of the Zoroastrian sacred literature concerns law in its various phases
and spheres. The conception of law proper in Zoroastrianism
is as old as the Avesta itself. The first person referred to
as a law codifier in Zoroastrianism is Urvaxšya,[1] the brother

---

1. Y.9, sec. 10. "yat hē puθra us.zayōiθe urvāxšayō kərəsaspasca;
    tkaēšo anyō dātō.razō āat anyō . . ." i.e., two sons were born
    to him [to θraētaona]: Urvaxšya and Keresāspa, one [the former]
    a teacher, lawgiver, and the other . . . ."

i

of Keresāspa and the son of Θraētaona, a descendant of
Yima, the first legendary king. When the Dēnkard, a middle
Persian encyclopedia of Zoroastrianism,[1] gives a summary
of the contents of the Avesta, it says:

> The divisions of the reckoning of the
> Mazda-worshipping revelation are three:
> gāsānīg, which is the higher spiritual
> knowledge and duty; dādīg (legal),
> which is mostly worldly knowledge and
> worldly duty; and hadā mānsrīg, which
> is mostly information and data about
> what is between these two.[2]

The Dēnkard goes on to explain the subdivisions of each
major division. One of the subdivisions of the law section
is the law book of Vendidād,[3] which along with an extensive
commentary in Pahlavi, survives as part of the Avesta.

The first law book per se in Pahlavi, Mādayān-i
Hazār Dādestān [Book of a Thousand Judgments], was composed
during the reign of Khosrow I (reigned A.D. 531-579), by

---

1. The work consists of twenty-one nasks (divisions) an order in
   which the twenty-one words of the Ahunavar (the most cardinal
   prayer of the Zoroastrians) are applied to the twenty-one
   nasks. The first compilation of this Zoroastrian religious
   encylopedia took place in the early ninth century by Ādur
   Farnbag-i Farróxzādan, and later in the early 10th century
   by Adurbād, son of Hēmīt.

2. DK., book VIII, chapter 1, sec. 5.

3. Pahlavi Vendidād is really a mis-reading of Vidēvdād, which
   corresponds to Av. vi + daēva + dāta, i.e., the law against
   evil spirits.

Farroxmard-i Wahrān. It is believed that this lengthy
codification of Zoroastrian law was a response to in-
creasing heretical beliefs. The M̄ādayān-i Hazār Dādestān[1]
is a genuine reflection of the social and ethical laws of
the late Sasanian period in Persia and claims to cover a
period between A.D. 399 and A.D. 628.

Another book containing religious and legal
matters compiled in the Pahlavi language is Dādestān-i
Dēnīg [Religious Judgments].[2] This book contains the
answers of Manusčihr. the high priest of Pars and Kirmān
(later half of the ninth century), to ninety-two questions
put to him by his coreligionists. It covers a broad range
of subjects including doctrinal matters, ethics, cosmology,
and the rights and duties of the priests. It also deals with
various social and legal points. This work reflects the
waning power and wealth of the Zoroastrian community of that era.

Next to these two books stand the Pahlavi and Persian
Rivāyats.

---

1. This book has been translated into English by S. J. Bulsara, a
    Parsi scholar, under the title The Laws of Ancient Persians as
    Found in "Mātikān-i Hazār Dātastān" (Bombay, 1937). A. Perikh-
    anian of Leningrad has prepared a Russian translation of the
    book, which in turn has been translated into English by Prof.
    N. Garsöian of Princeton University but not yet published.
    C. Bartholomae in a series of lengthy articles has discussed
    some passages of this book under the title "Notes on Sasanian
    Law," transl. by L. Bogdanov, Cama Oriental Institute Publica-
    tion (Bombay, 1931-1967).

2. The complete translation of this book is given by E. W. West
    in SBE. XVIII.

The Pahlavi Rivāyats

The word Rivāyat is not used in Pahlavi
texts. It appears that the word Rivāyat was applied
to those Pahlavi writings at a later date. The Rivāyats
were compiled or composed approximately during the later
part of the ninth century A.D. or early part of the tenth
century A.D. They are based on Pahlavi translations of
the Avesta and other Pahlavi books extant in those days.
These Pahlavi Rivāyats known at present, composed by various authors, are:

a) The Rivāyat accompanying (in the manuscript
   of) the Dādestān-i Dēnīg.

b) The Rivāyat of Hēmīt-i Ašawahištān.

c) The Rivāyats of Ādūrfarnbag and Farnbag
   Srōš.

d) The Rivāyat based on Pahlavi Vidēvdād--
   a Pahlavi text of questions and answers
   on various religious subjects on the authority of the Pahlavi Vidēvdād.[1]

---

1. The importance of Pahlavi Vidēvdād is that not only is it
   a genuine translation of the Avestan one, but it is full of
   added Pahlavi commentaries which makes it more documentary
   from the legal viewpoint.

·Persian Rivāyats

Between the fifteenth and seventeenth centuries
A.D. the Parsi priests of India sent emissaries to Iran,
and addressed a number of inquiries on religion, ceremonies,
scriptures, customs and practices to the priests in Iran.
Lengthy and detailed replies thereto were received from time
to time, and the literature thus formed of these questions
and replies is termed Rivāyat. The first Rivāyat was brought
in 1478 A.D. by one Nariman Hushang, a resident of Broach.
This Rivāyat is known by his name: The Rivāyat of Nariman
Hushang. Similarly, other Rivāyats are known for the person
who brought them. Some are anonymous, as the persons who
brought them are unknown. During the course of three centuries (fifteenth through seventeent A.D.) about twenty-one
Rivāyats were collected and classified according to subject
matter, by Hormazdyār Farāmarz, Dārāb Hormazdyār and Barno
Kāmdīn (all members of a very distinguished and learned
family). The classified Rivāyats are known after them. The
collection of the classified Rivāyats was prepared by
M. R. Unvala and was published after Unvala's death in a
lithograph edition by J. J. Modi, Bombay, in 1922. They
were translated into English with an introduction and copious
notes by B. N. Dhabhar, Bombay, in 1932, under the title
The Persian Rivāyats of Hormazdyār Farāmarz and Others.[1]

---

1. H. K. Mirza, OPH., pp. 301 and 310.

Through the Persian Rivāyats we learn not only about
the rituals and customs of the Zoroastrians but also the
history of Zoroastrianism in the Islamic era.

Rivāyat-i Hēmīt-i Ašawahištān

Among the Pahlavi Rivāyats referred to above
(p. iv) the one by Hēmīt-i Ašawahištān, the subject of
this book, is of great importance.

Hēmīt, son of Ašawahišt, belonged to a learned
family of Zoroastrian priests who flourished in the ninth
century A.D. In the Pahlavi literature, Zurvandād, Manusčihr, Zādspram, Farnbag and Hēmīt are mentioned as religious heads and literary personages, "pēšopāy-i dēn,"
leaders of the religion. The genealogy of Hēmīt is given
in detail by B. T. Anklesaria in Selections of Zādspram
(Bombay, 1964), Introduction p. xv, and also in the introduction of R.F.S. p. 21, and BTE. p. 3. According to Arabic
writers of the twelfth century A.D. Hēmīt is referred to
as امید بن اشوشت "Amid Ībn-i Ašavašt" and is titled as
موبدان موبد "Mobadān Mobad."[1]

Although the Rivāyats all deal with the religious
laws and principles prevailing in Persia during the Sasanian

---

1. J. J. Modi, "The Mōbadān Mōbad امید بن اشوشت referred to by
Hamzeh Isfehani," Studia Indo Iranica (Otto Harrassowitz,
Leipzig, 1931), pp. 275-288.

and immediate post-Sasanian eras, the <u>Rivāyat</u> of Hēmīt
differs in several important aspects from the others.
For one thing, it does not contain the usual introductory
epistles found in most <u>Rivāyats</u>. Also absent are the
ornate style and conjectures common in the traditional
<u>Rivāyats</u>. It seems that Hēmīt, high priest of Pars and
Kirman (c. 950 A.D.), was primarily concerned with a
straightforward presentation of legal and ritual prescriptions rather than the niceties of textual ornamenta-
tion and erudite theological speculation.

Hēmīt's <u>Rivāyat</u> was composed in about the tenth
century A.D. (the earliest manuscript extant of this <u>Rivāyat</u>
belongs to the early seventeenth century) when Zoroastrianism
was threatened with extinction through voluntary as well as
compulsory conversion of its adherents to other faiths,
primarily Islam. Accordingly, in both content and structure
the <u>Rivāyat-i Hēmīt</u> reflects the urgency of the need to
reinforce Zoroastrian dogma and practices in the face of
the Moslem domination of Persia and the undermining of the
old value system. The limited focus of the questions presented in the <u>Rivāyat-i Hēmīt</u>, with their emphasis on social
and religious status, inheritance, rights, and family relationships among those followers who had converted, indicates
that the broad, more theoretical concessions contained in
earlier writings were not perceived to be effective in

hindering the disintegration of the community and the
Zoroastrian faith and were therefore unsuitable for
the circumstances.

The forty-four queries and answers comprising
the Rivāyat-i Hēmīt can justifiably be classed with the
other two major Persian law books written in Pahlavi,
Mādayān-i Hazār Dādestān and Dādestān-i Dēnīg, whose
presentation of various legal-social regulations as well
as the rights and duties of the priests are almost identical. The following sample passages from the above mentioned
law books will illustrate the point.

From the Mh.D. facsimile edition T.D. Anklesaria,
Bombay, 1912:

Dar-i guft abāg guft (p. 88 v. 5th sentence)

ud ān-ē guft kū pasēmāl tā dādestān az
rāyēnišn mānēd pad guft dādestān pēsēmāl
hamēmālīh kardan nē pādixšā.abāg ān-ē
guft kū ka andar rāyēnišn-i dādestān pus
purnāy bawēd dūdag sālār dādestān
rāyēnīdan nē tuwān ud pasēmāl pādixšā ka
dūdag sālār az rāyēnišn be ne hilēd ud
ham pacēn stānēd ud pad wad xwāh andar
dūdag sālār nū nē pēsēmāl andar dūdag
sālār ēd dādestān az rāyēnišn mānēd.

Chapter on Consultation

And another [sentence] runs that, as
long as a decision remains to be given
regarding [a case at] court, the defendant
can not claim counter case as plaintiff.
Also another [sentence] runs that while the
law suit is in progress, should a son reach

maturity, the family guardian can not
proceed with the case and it would be
legal for the defendant to move to have
the case dismissed and take possession of
the papers and demand judgement, regarding
the family guardian for malice, because
the guardian is now no longer plaintiff
and this law suit [in effect] terminates.

And from the Dd. etition, T. D. Anklesaria,
Bombay, 1934:

Chap. 9 (p. 26)

1. nohom pursišn ān i pursēd kū waxš-i
    kirbag-ē az ān-i ka kirbag ēstēd tā
    ān-i ka zindag čand abzāyēd.

2. passox ēd kū az ān-i ke kirbag be ō
    rawāgīh rasēd waxš andar ō abzāyišn
    jahēd tā ka zindag.bē ka-š ān-ē kirbag
    uš be ačārēhēd tā waxš-i waxš abāz nē
    ēstēd.ēdōn waxšēd čiyōn frazand andar
    aškamb-i mādarān abzāyēd bawēd.

1. The ninth question inquires: To what
    extent the generation of a meritorious
    deed increases, from the moment it is
    performed as long as [the performer]
    lives.

2. The answer is: from the moment a
    meritorious deed is put into effect,
    as long as [the performer] lives its
    generation will ever increase. Further,
    even if that meritorious deed causes
    him distress, while increase after
    increase will not cease, it grow in
    the same manner that a child grows in
    the womb of the mother.

The main difference is that <u>Mādayān-i Hazār Dādestān</u> and

<u>Dādestān-i Dēnīg</u> were composed at a much earlier period

ix

(A.D. 596 and 881 respectively) and were concerned with
a broad range of legal problems and issues that had
developed naturally over time as the society grew and the
modes of social interaction became more complex. This is
especially true of the Mādayān, whose general, almost
leisurely style and method of presentation contrasts sharp-
ly with the urgency reflected in the rigorous precision and
conciseness of the forty-four queries comprising the
Rivāyat-i Hēmīt.

         The style of Rivāyat-i Hēmīt is direct and compact;
the questions are dogmatic, not maieutic. They are answered
very precisely, stressing the most vital points whose
neglect would have had a direct effect on Zoroastrian
community life in terms of religious prescriptions and
would eventually have been a sign of disrespect toward the
accurate practice of the religious laws. These are laws of
a practical religion which emphasize the free will of
individuals, a religion which is based on good thoughts,
good words and good deeds, a religion which provides practical guidance to people who are involved in business and
government as well as spiritual matters.

         A point of great interest is that the Rivāyat-i Hēmī
and other Pahlavi texts were composed as early as the ninth
century A.D. yet we know from statements in the Persian
Rivāyat of Nariman Hushang (written A.D. 1474) that Pahlavi

was still the religious language of the Zoroastrian priests
in Iran and that there remained a few hērbeds who were
well versed in that language, and that it was an absolute
prerequisite for a well-versed priest to know the language,
since most of the religious texts and rituals were in
Pahlavi. This fact shows that even as late as nine hundred
years after the Islamic conquest of Persia, Pahlavi, which
had been the official language of the Sasanians, was still
in use on at least some occasions for religious purposes.

          The question and answer pattern of Rivāyat-i Hēmīt
is a traditional form dating back to the Gāthas. A few
examples are Y. 29, 31, 34, 43, 44. In Y. 44, nineteen times
this same phrase is repeated by Zarathushtra: "That which
I ask you tell me soon Oh Ahura Mazdah" to which he receives
replies respectively either through revelation or direct
answers. In Y. 43 Zarathushtra repeatedly tells us that by
means of vohu manah (divine intelligence) he reached Ahura
Mazdah and became conversant with him in the affairs of
both material and spiritual world. He also says that such
inspiration is not a monopoly and in order to receive direct
guidance   for every problem one should ask questions
from Ahura Mazdah and receive answers through concentration
and meditation. There is a reference to this remark in
Vd. 18-13, where Ahura Mazdah addresses Zarathushtra: "Ask
questions from me who am the creator, the bringer of prosperity,

omniscient and giver of replies to questions. It will

benefit you by asking me questions. You will become

more wise by asking me questions."

The complete account of the meeting of Zara-

thushtra with Ahura Mazdah (as given in Y. 43) and all

their conversation is given to us at length in the Persian

Zardušt Nāmeh.

These were a few examples of questions and answers

in Gāthas. The same principle is reflected in Vendidād.

> " Vendidād   has been often compared with
> that of the Book of Moses. But in
> reality, in the Bible, there is no con-
> versation between God and the lawgiver:
> The law comes down unasked, and God gives
> commands, but gives no answers. In the
> Vendidād, on the contrary it is the wish
> of man not the will of God that is the
> first cause of revelation. Man must ask
> of Ahura who knows everything and is
> pleased to answer; the law is 'the
> question to Ahura ' (Ahuri frašnō)." [1]

Also the same pattern has been carried out through

Zoroastrian religious books written in Pahlavi language.

Examples are:

. Dādestān-i Dēnīg, referred to above, p. iii)

. Yošt-i Fryān, which is initially a religious text

but is considered rather a popular riddle-wisdom literature.

---

1.   SBE. vol. IV, Introd. lxxxv, note 4.

It comprises the riddles posed by Axt, a sorcerer, to
Yošt, a righteous man whose life depended on his resolving
the riddles.

. <u>Draxt-i Asurīg</u>, which is also a wisdom literature
based on religious concepts in a dialogue form between a
palm tree and a goat.

. <u>Menōg-i xrad</u> (Judgment of the Spirit of Wisdom), in
which the questioner seeks to establish the truth of Zoroastrianism and receives replies from the spirit of wisdom.

. <u>Namagīhā-i Manuščihr</u> (epistles of Manuščihr) whose
author is the same as that of <u>Dādestān-i Dēnīg</u>. It is
another example of Pahlavi literature of the seventh-ninth
century A.D. in dialogue form. The Pahlavi and Persian
<u>Rivāyats</u> of later centuries (fourteenth-seventeenth centu-
ries A.D.) also fall in the same category of dialogue pattern
style.

The Manuscript

The manuscript of <u>Rivāyat-i Hēmīt</u> makes up a section of a whole collection of Pahlavi manuscripts written by Frētōn Marzbān in c. 1629 A.D., a possession of B. T. Anklesaria's library. This manuscript comprises Pahlavi texts of:

. Bundahišn (fo. 2-122).

. a few lines of Persian poetry (fo. 122).

. <u>Rivāyat-i Hēmīt</u> (fo. 123-163). See below, N.B.

. 147 questions required of Adūr Farnbag-i Farrox-Zādān (fo. 163-203).

. The four questions inquired of Farnbag Srōš-i Wahrān with date of its composition (fo. 203-206).

. The 30 questions inquired of Mowbedān Mowbed (fo. 206-212).

. A brief description of the system of purification (fo. 212-213).

. The vicīrīhā-i dēn-i vēh-i Mazdayasnān (fo. 213-218).

. The Commentary of Vendidād (fo. 218-327).

. The Pursišnīhā (fo. 327-354).

. A Colophon in Pahlavi (fo. 354-).

. The Avesta Pahlavi text of Afrīn-i Zarathušt (fo. 354-3?

. The incomplete Pahlavi Pāzand Glossary (fo. 359- onwards)

N.B.: It was published for the first time in 1962 by

J. C. Tarapore at the request of Mrs. M. B. Anklesaria
by permission of the University of Bombay for the Cama
Oriental Institute, Bombay.

The Pahlavi text was prepared by the late B. T.
Anklesaria as a prize essay for the University of Bombay
in 1928. The university resolved to publish the text along
with the English translation and transcription, but because
of various difficulties, the work remained unpublished
during the lifetime of B. T. Anklesaria. In 1945, while
the work was being printed by the Fort Printing Press,
Bombay, a disastrous fire destroyed all copies. The offset
copy which is now available has been published as volume I
of the work with transcription by B. T. Anklesaria along
with notes on the emendations made by him of the manuscript.
The translation of the text with copious notes which was
to appear as volume II has remained unpublished. B. T.
Anklesaria had prepared the text from the above mentioned
collection of manuscripts belonging to his father, T. D.
Anklesaria. N. B. Dhabhar has mentioned one other manuscript
of this text found by him in Mulla Firuz Library, now housed
in Cama Oriental Institute, which he describes on p. 35 of
his Catalogue as "a very fair copy of the old manuscript of
the Rivāyat, the property of T. D. Anklesaria, but is incomplete at the end and is written by Dastur Mehrjirana."

Dhabhar adds that a complete copy of this rare manuscript was made by Dastur Erachji and is preserved in the Navsari Library. Thus far only a few fragmentary excerpts from this work have been translated by Jean De Menasce, K. M. JamaspAsa and K. Kanga, to which references are made in detail in the following transcriptions and translations of the text.

Summary of the Contents of the Questions

in Rivāyat-i Hēmīt

Q. 1.   Social status of a married woman in relation with
          her brother's conversion to Islam.

Q. 2.   If a married woman's social status is going to be
          affected by her brother's conversion, would it
          affect the conditions of the children of the
          woman in question?

Q. 3.   What is the domain of a lady of a family regarding
          her full authority over the wealth left behind by
          her husband?

Q. 4.   What are the legal prescriptions regarding inheri-
          tance of a converted son?

Q. 5.   Different types of family guardianship.

Q. 6.   What should be the qualifications of a family
          guardian? What are the procedures of his appoint-
          ment?

Q. 7.   What would be the situation of a woman if her
          husband deprives her of inheritance? What is the
          status of a collateral wife?

Q. 8.   Can a man forbid the assignment of a proxy for his
          family?

Q. 9.   What would be the situation of a teacher-priest
          when he does not do his job properly?

Q. 10.   Can a teacher-priest join the military?

Q. 11.   If a teacher-priest joins the military would he
          be admitted to priesthood afterwards?

Q. 12.   What would be the situation of a teacher-priest if
          he undertakes the ritual of purification when he
          is not yet qulified to do so?

Q. 13.   What should a man or a woman do if there is no
          access to a purifier?

A Brief Note on the Translation

of Pahlavi

Pahlavi was the official language of the Sasanian
period. Geographically its origin was in southwestern Iran,
and it is a member of the Iranian language group. The fact
that its alphabet, derived from the Aramaic alphabet, indicates only consonants and long vowels makes it very difficul
to decipher. In the cursive Pahlavi of the Zoroastrian text
certain characters stand for more than one sound, an easy
source of misreadings unless one is quite sure of the context. Although Pahlavi is a purely Iranian language, its
written form included many Aramaic heterograms, frozen forms
that serve as symbols for the Iranian equivalent, although
written in Aramaic. For example, "to die" is written
YMYTWN-tn (the suffix -dan [written tn] is the Iranian
infinitive ending) but is read murdan. This practice is not
analogous to the use of Latin abbreviations as symbols in
English, such as viz. or lb., because viz. is a conventional
abbreviation of the Latin vide licit and lb. of libra. The
Aramaic heterograms were used in Pahlavi in their full
written form, just as they would be in an Aramaic text.
There is also a sharp difference between the usage of pre-
Islamic Semitic words in Pahlavi and that of post-Islamic

ones. The former never became part of the language.
By contrast, the post-Islamic Semitic words used in
Farsi (modern Persian) became a part of the language.
They kept their original pronunciation in Farsi (with
modifications in Persian pronunciation). They comprised
all religious words and expressions, and if taken out
of the sentence and replaced by an Iranian counterpart,
the context would sound out of form.[1]

The complexity of the Pahlavi language has in-
hibited the translation of many of all the Pahlavi texts
that exist. Many of those which have been translated are
either done very freely in order to be understandable or
are as difficult to understand as the original text would
be for someone who is not familiar with the Pahlavi language.
In the present translation I have tried to maintain fidelity
to the text even in terms of word order, though I have
supplied twentieth-century assumptions to determine the
correct translation. If certain parts have seemed inconsistent
in the text, I have chosen the most likely alternative (in
complete context in the footnotes). For example, in ans. 1,
sec. 4 and ans. 7, sec. 8 regarding the word اویدرم‌ا which
Anklesaria has read viptan, I have suggested nigēxtan, meaning
to disclose, to expose.

---

1.   For references to the Pahlavi language see the bibliography.

xxi

Guiding Notes on the Text

In all instances I have followed the principles
of Pahlavi transcription established by D. N. MacKenzie
in his dictionary, excepting the case of the title of
the book and the name of the author. The reason is
that the only extant edited version of the manuscript
by B. T. Anklesaria, himself an eminent Parsi scholar
in Pahlavi studies, bears the traditional transcription
reflecting the familiar pronunciation of the name.
Besides, this would be the spelling used in all card
catalogues.

See also MacKenzie's "Notes on the Transcription of
Pahlavi," BSOAS., XXX, Pt. 1 (1967), pp. 17-29.

The text and translation are here arranged so
that the sections of the transcriptions and
translations are the same on each page to make
reference to the text easier.

Rivāyat-i Hēmīt-i Ašawahištān

0) pad nām-i dādār-i weh-i abzōnīg-i kirbakkar.

1) ēn pursišnīhā-ē čand az hūfraward Hēmīt -i Ašawahištān pursēd man Ādur Gušnasp-1 Mihr Ātaxš-i Ādur Gušnasp. andar farroxīh mān-i warzāwand ātaxš.

2) kašēd az pačēn-i anōšag-i farrox.

3) hūdahišn bawād.

Rivāyat-i Hēmīt-i Ašawahištān

0) In the name of the good, bountiful, beneficent Creator.

1) I, Ādur Gušnasp-i Mihr Ādūr Gušnasp, in the blessed Temple
of the glorious fire, asked a few questions from the
venerable Hēmīt-i Ašawahištān.

2) [The questions were] compiled from the everlasting
blessed scripture.

3) May it be [of service as] a good donation.[1]

---

1. The last two sentences could be divided in two otherwise arranged
sentences which would be equally possible, i.e., a) the questions were adapted from the scripture [i.e., Avesta]. b) May he
[Hēmīt] be immortal, fortunate, and of divine favour. The last sentence, the subject of which would be Hēmīt [who had clarified the problems with his answers] is a very common complimentary phrase found in
Pahlavi texts when the name of a revered deceased person is mentioned.
The division would be as the following:

   a) kašēd az pačēn.
   b) i anōsag-i farrox hudahišn bawād.

pursišn 1

1) mard-ē būd.uš zan-ē būd i pādixša.pus dō.duxt do ō
   dād-i pānzdah sāl rasēd hēnd.pus ēk ō ōh gyāg bēgānagīh
   šud.ēk az āwām šud.ušān duxt ō šōy dād.pas az sāl
   dranāy duxt kē-š šōy kard būd az-š pus-ē zād būd.āgāhīh
   mad ku ān mard kē pad bēgānagīh būd.pēš az be dādan im
   duxt ō šōy.az dād-i weh dēnīh ō dād-i akdēnīh šud būd.

2) nūn dādestān-i im duxt čē.pad pādixšā zanīh-i im mard
   i šōy hast.ayāb ayōkēn stūr-i dūdag hast.

Question 1

1) There was a man who had a pādixšā [1] wife, two sons, two
daughters, who had reached the age of fifteen. One of
the sons went to a foreign city. The other one passed
away. They [i.e., the parents] gave away their daughter
to a husband. After the period of one year, the married
daughter gave birth to a son. News came that the man
who was in a foreign city prior to his sister's marriage
had been converted from wehdēn [2] to akdēn. [3]

2) Now, what is the situation of this girl? Does she remain
the pādixšā wife of her husband, or [under these circum-
stances] does she become ayōkēn [4] stūr [5] of her family?

---

1. She is independent, with full authority regarding her children.
   She is only dependent on her husband in respect of food and clothing.
   She can become the family guardian after her husband's death. For
   more details see: R.FS. tr. Ank. p. 42; R.HF. pp. 195 and 197;
   also Sd.Bd. chap. 87, of R.HF. p. 564.

2. Zoroastrian religion, lit. "the good religion."

3. Islam: See Men. "La Rivāyat d'Emēt i Ašavahištan," Revue de l'Histoire des Religions (Paris, 1962), p. 76. Also see Appendix below for
   comments of H.K. Mirza on the word akdēn.

4. She who has no father or brother. For more details see R.FS. tr.
   Ank. p. 44; R.HF. pp. 195 and 198; also see below ans. 31, sec. 8.

5. A proxy, guardian, also an adoptive son. For details see R.HF.
   p. 179, 186; C. Bartholomae, NSL. (1931), XVIII, 21; A. Perikhanian,
   "On Some Pahlavi Legal Terms," W.B. Henning memorial vol. (London:
   Lund Humphries, 1970), pp. 353-7; M. Boyce, Letter of Tansar (Rome:
   UNESCO Publications, 1968), p. 46. Also see Mansour Shaki, "The
   Concept of Obligated Successorship in the Mādiyān-i Hazār Dādistān,"
   Monumentum H. S. Nyberg (Acta-Iranica, 1975), pp. 227-242.

passox 1

3) agar-š čiš andar nēst ān rāy juttar,brād.kē az āwām
šud.rāy zan ud frazand pādixšā ayāb pus-i padīraftag
ēk stūr-i kard hast.im duxt pad pādixšā zanīh-i im šōy
ēstēd.uš ayōkēnīh stūrīh-i any kas nēst.agarš zan ud
frazand pādixšāīhā.pus padīraftag ud stūr-i kardag ayāb
gumārdag nēst.im duxt pad ayōkēnīh stūr-i brād ēstēd.uš
padixšā zanīh im šōy nēst.pus i-š az-š zād andar dūdag-i
im brād zād bawēd.

4) agar im mard.kē-š šōy hast.sahēd kū im zan pad zanīh
dārēd.ēg-š pad ayōkēnīh brād zan abāyēd kardan.nigēzidan[1]
pad zanīh šōyīh dēnīgīhā xūb bawēd.ka juttar ēg nē xūb.
čē.im mard im zan pad pādixšāīhā.zanīh dāštan nē pādixšāī

---

1. BTE. اورکرد۱۱۳   Ank.reads viptan . For MS. see plate; see
also note 3, same translation.

Answer 1

3) If there is nothing else implied in the question which
would require another answer, if the brother who has
passed away has a padixšā wife or an offspring or
an adopted son or has a stūr kardag,[1] this girl remains
as padixšā wife for her husband and she will not become ayōkēn of anybody. If there is no padixšā wife
or any offspring or an adopted son or a stūr kardag or
gumārdag[2] left for him [i.e., the deceased brother],
this girl becomes ayōkēn stūr of her brother and is no
more the padixšā wife of her husband, and the son who is
born to her belongs to the lineage of her brother.

4) If this man who is her husband still wants to have her
as his wife, then while she is under his brother's
ayōkēnīh, he [the husband] must declare[3] his ayōkēnīh
marital status with her as approved by the doctrine of
husband and wife relationship. If otherwise, then it is
not lawful, because he has not the right to have her as
padixšā wife.

---

1. stūr-i kardag: see note on guardianship and adoption. below.

2. stūr-i gumārdag: idem.

3. See note 1 transl. ans. **7** sec. 8.

passox 1, cont'd

5)   ud agar dānēd kū pad pādixšāīhā zanīh dāštan nē
     dastwarīhā.uš pad pādixšāīhā dārēd pad gyāg tanāpuhl
     wināh.ud pad sāl dranāy margarzān.

6)   hamē ka be dānēd kū-š pādixšāīhā zanīh dāštan nē
     dastwarīhā.uš pad zanīh abāyišnīg.ēg-š zamānīg pad
     ayōkēnīh-i brād ud čagarzanīh zan kunišn.uš pad ayōkēnī-
     brād dārišn.az wināh abarnibišt abēzār.

Answer 1, cont'd.

5) If the husband knows that having her as padixša wife

is unlawful, and yet keeps her as that, he has committed

a tanāpuhl[1] sin immediately, and if he remains in that

sin for a year, then his sin becomes margarzān.[2]

6) If he is aware that having her as padixša wife is

not lawful, but wishes to have her as a wife, then for

the certain period of time that she is under the ayōkēnīh

of her brother, he must have marital relationship with

her only on the basis of a čagar[3] wife. Thus he will be

freed from the above-mentioned sins.

---

1. tanāpuhl: a sin which disables the sinner from passing činwad bridge (the bridge which leads the virtuous to heaven on the Day of Judgement), and whose atonement is 300 stīrs (a unit of money). R.HF. p. 289.

2. margarzān: a sin for which there is no atonement, and death is the punishment for it.

3. čagar wife: If a woman is married and her husband dies, and if this woman is remarried, then she is a čagar of her former husband, and she belongs to her former husband in that world who has a share in her children by her second husband. R.HF. p. 195; "collateral wife", Bartholomae, NSL., XVIII, 36.

N.B. Guardianship and adoption: "It is said that there are three kinds: (1) the existent (būtak), (2) the provided (kartak) and (3) the appointed (gūmārtak)." For full details see: R.HF. pp. 186-7.

"There are two kinds of guardians 'gōmārta' appointed and 'būta' become. The appointed guardian of a woman can not hand her over in guardianship to another in the same manner that a 'become' could. A guardian who is a 'become' can hand over a woman who is in his ward in guardianship to a man. He could also make a woman who is his ward, independent guardian of her own self." For more details, see R.FS. tr. Ank. pp. 38-39. Also, see ans. 5, sec. 2-3.

Appendix Question 1

Dr. H. K. Mirza's Comments on the Word akdēn

The manuscript <u>TD2</u> and <u>G</u> are described by T. D. Anklesaria in the <u>Pahlavi Rivāyat of Aturfarnbag and Farnbag-Sroš</u>, introduction pages 25-31.

<u>juddēn</u>:   "A person of an alien religion," generally applied to a non-Zoroastrian.

<u>anēr</u>:   "A non-Iranian," generally refers to an Arab.

<u>anērīh</u>:   "Non-Iranianism,"generally used for the religion of the Arabs, Islam.

<u>akdēn</u>:   "A person of bad religion or wrong religion," generally applied to a Zoroastrian convert to Islam.

    Av. a**ǰ**adaēna "bad religion," Vd. 18,9. According to this Av. passage, that person teaches "bad religion" who does not put on sacred thread, who does not offer prayers as applied to a Zoroastrian. Hence "bad religion" means discarding one's own Zoroastrian religion and instigating others to do so.

    Furthermore, in Vd. 3,40. Av. anāstutō, Pahlavi tr. <u>an-astavān</u> "one without faith, [in Zoroastr. religion]", and it is explained in a gloss: akdēn.

    This is corroborated by <u>Dēnkard</u>, edited by D. M. Madan, p. 201, lines 8-10:

        abāč stāyitan, hangirdīk dō ēvēnak: ahrmanīk čigōn an-hast mēnītan akdēnīk čigōn a-veh mēnītan-i vēhdēn.

        "Discarding the praise [of Zoroastrian religion] is generally of two categories: [one] Satanic (<u>ahrmanīk</u>), such as to consider [the religion] as non-existent, [and the second] of bad religion (<u>akdēn</u>), such as to consider the Good Religion (<u>vēhdēn</u>) [Zoroastrian] as not good."

Appendix Question 1, cont'd.

Here heresy, not believing in any religion,
is regarded as "satanic, demonic", and consi-
dering one's own Zoroastrian religion as "not
good", and hence adopting an alien religion,
is regarded as an act "pertaining to bad religion".

This clearly shows that Pahlavi akdēn,"a person of bad religion", is a Zoroastrian convert
to Islam.

pursišn 2

1) agar im duxt ayōkēn stūr-i[1] dūdag hast.pad rāh-i
    ayōkēnīh ud stūrīh-i dūdag.xwāstag i andar im dūdag be
    ō duxt frazand rasēd ayāb nē.

passox 2

2) agar-š čiš andar nēst ān rāy juttar.brād-i weh dēn-i[2]
    az āwām šudag.rāy zan ud frazand pādixšāīh.pus-i
    padīraftag.stūr kardag. ayōk-iz nēst.az im čim.dādestanīh
    im xwahar hast kū pad ayōkēnīh brādar ēstēd.xīr ud
    xwāstag pad xwēšīh im brād ēstēd.hamāg pad ayōkēnīh-i
    brād bē ō im xwahar rasēd.uš pad ayōkēnīh ud stūrīh brād
    dārišn.ēdōn-iz abārīg xwāstag andar im dūdag-iz.

---

1. Not in BTE., nor in the MS.

2. Not in BTE., nor in the MS.

Question 2

1) If this girl is [remains] ayōkēn of the family according to [the law of] ayōkēn stūrīh as practiced in the
family, would her child inherit any property of this
family?

Answer 2

2) If there is nothing else implied in the question which
would require another answer; if the deceased brother
was an adherent of the Zoroastrian religion, and did
not have a pādixšā wife or any offspring, or an adopted
son or an appointed trustee, nor an ayōkēn, then under the
circumstances, according to jurisprudence, this sister
remains under the brother's ayōkēnīh. [Thus] property
and wealth would go to her brother. Eventually because
of her being ayōkēn of her brother, all that property
would go to this sister [after his death]. And she would
possess this [wealth] through being her brother's ayōkēn
and stūr. Likewise [this applies to] other properties
which are also in this family.

pursišn 3

1) Agar ān zan dūdag kadag bānūg būd ud mādar-i im
   frazandān bud.čiš-ē čiyōn payrāyag-i tan ud bahrpā.i-š
   az šoy rasēd.eg-š ō duxt dād.pad duxt pādixšā būd ayāb
   nē.

Question 3

1) Assume a woman who is her family's lady of the house[1]
    and who also has children, if her husband passes away
    and leaves to her certain things such as body or foot
    adornment, if she gives [anything] to her daughter,
    would she [the daughter] be entitled to that [posses-
    sion] or not?

---

1. A position similar to that of   pādixšā wife.

passox 3

2) ka čiš andar nēst ān rāy juttar.ka kadag xwadāy
widardag stūr ne[1] hamē gumārd zamānag dādan-i[2] dūdag
kadag bānūg ō har kas ke xwāhēd dahēd.rawāg.

3) pas.ka ēd kū dādestan be ō ān rasēd kū kadag xwadāy
stūr abāyēd gumārdan.andar dūdag.kē stūr pad-š šāyēd
gumardan.jud az ān i dūdag kadag bānūg [be dādan[3]]
nēst.ān i dūdag kadagbānūg be dād. ō har kē-š dād.uš
xwāstag sē stīr-i barōmand abāz āwarišn.kadag xwadāy
stūr pad-š gumārišn.

---

1. BTE. rā. See plate .

2. Ank. reads "dāt". See plate.

3. I believe this bē dadan which I have put in brackets must be an
an erroneous interpolation.

Answer 3

2) If there is nothing else implied in the question which
would require another answer, when the master of a house
passes away and a proxy is not appointed within "proper
period[1] of time", it is lawful for the lady of the house
to give [anything] to anybody she wants.

3) Then, if the situation legally comes to a point that
the lord of the house must have had appointed a proxy
in the family for which a proxy should have been assigned,
and since that proxy could not have been other than the
lady of the house,[2] [therefore] she is entitled to give
[anything] to anybody she desires so. [But] she must
refund from that property an amount of three interest-
bearing stir,[3] to which the master of the house should
have assigned a proxy.[4]

---

1. zamānag: a guardian should be appointed within a year. Dd. tr.
    Dh.R.HF. p. 186.

2. Dd. chap. 53.9 tr. R.HF. p. 190

3. "It is a weight of 6-1/2 dirham, each dirham is a silver coin general-
    ly in value about 2 pence sterling." R.HF. p. 56. "The regular sala-
    ry of a proxy is 4 setir per month." Ibid., p. 187.

4. See ans. 18, sec. 7.

17

passox 3, cont'd.

4) agar kadag xwadāy rāy stūr nē hamē abāyēd gumārd.ayāb
dūdag xwāstag-i kē stūr pad-š šāyēd gumārdan.az ān
gumārišn ān i dūdag kadag bānūgīg pad xwešīh ō duxt ayāb
any kas dād. čiyōn-š dād šud.abāz nē āwarišn.pad ōy kē
awiš dād be ēstēd.

5) agar pas dādestān-i im duxt ōwōn bawēd kū-š stūrīh
dūdag be ō duxt dād.abārīg čē andar dūdāg hast.hamāg be
ō duxt rasēd uš pad stūrīh-i dūdag dārišn.

Answer 3, cont'd.

4) If there is no need to assign a proxy for the master
    of the house or the family property to which a proxy
    should be assigned, from that assignment it [the right
    of curation] goes to the possession of the lady of the
    house; she is allowed to give to her daughter or to any-
    body else [what she wants]. But the moment she gives
    it, she has no right to take it back. So from that
    very moment, that property remains the personal belong-
    ing of the person to whom it has been given [i.e., the
    daughter].

5) If later the status of this daughter legally requires
    that she should become the proxy of the family, then
    [that portion allocated to the daughter by her mother plus]
    the rest of the property of the family goes to her, and [she]
    should keep it in 'curatorship.'

pursišn 4

1)   pus akdēn.har ān i-š az pidar ud mādar pad weh dēnīh

   rasēd.ēg-š pad akdēnīh bawēd ayāb nē.

Question 4

1) [Suppose] a son has become a Moslem [akdēn]. Is the
   right of property owenership, regarding the belongings
   he has received from his parents while he was a Zoroastrian, still effective despite his conversion?

passox 4

2) mard kē az weh dēnīh ō akdēnīh šawēd.ud pad akdēnīh be
rasēd.pad gyāg tanāpuhl-ē wināh.ka andar sāl dranāy pad
rāh-i weh dēn   hilēd margarzān.

3) agar-š pad handām droš.i čīyōn akdēnān pad kardag
dārēnd.kunēd.ud ān i-š az handām burēnd.ō āb ud ātaxš.
andar zamīg nihānīh.rasēd.ēg kamest margarzān wīnāh
bawēd.[1]

4) agar-š xwāstag-ē.hamāg pad paoiryāi   dāmanąm ēstēd.

5) paoiryāi   dāmanąm wizārišn ēn kū.az wēh dēnān har kē
ān xwāstag fradom abar girēd.ēg-š xwēš-rawišnīh pad-š
pādixšāīhā.

6) andar ēn awām.ēn ēwēnag kardan dušwār.ka šāyēd kardan.az
pēš rawēd.kardan dastwarīhā.čē ēn nē čīyōn ōy kē-š
akdēnīh az abarmand.

---

1.   I think the word order after the word akdēnān to the word ēg
should be amended to: pad kardag kunēnd.ud an i-š az handām burēnd
andar zamīg nihānīh dārēnd.ō āb ud ātaxs rasēd, which I have translated accordingly.

Answer 4

2) If a man converts from Zoroastrianism to Islam, and
   remains Moslem, he would be immediately considered as
   a tanāpuhl sinner. If within a year he does not turn
   towards Zoroastrianism, then his sin would be margarzān.

3) If [he has received] a brand on an organ of his body,
   as the Moslems do on a[n especial] section [of their body],
   and that which they cut from the organ they dispose of by
   covering it out of sight in the earth, [but eventually]
   reaches the fire and the water [polluting them], in that
   case the least grade of his sin is margarzān.

4) If he possesses any property, the law of the primitive
   men would apply to it.

5) The explanation of the law of primitive men is whoever
   from among the Zoroastrians first seizes it, is entitled
   to it.

6) In our era this is difficult to practice. If circumstances require that this step should be taken, and if it
   is carried out successfully, it would be considered lawful, because his case is different from he who is Moslem
   by heritage.

<u>passox 4</u>, cont'd.

7) pus-i akdēn ka sāl dranāy pad akdēnīh ēstēd.uš abāz
    nē[1] dārēd.andar dūdag-i pidar xwāstag hast.kē ān akdēn
    bahr az-š nē stad ēstēd.ēg-š im xwāstag hamāg appār.ud
    pad ān gōnag ēsted abar nibišt. im xwāstag-i wehdēn.ka-šā
    tuwān kū bahr-ē ōy-i akdēn pad <u>paoiryāi   dāmanąm</u> girēnd.
    pad xwēšīh-i xwēš dārēnd.ud ō akdēn nē dahēnd.pādixšā hēn
    ušān stāndan dastwarīhā.

8) ud agar im ēwēnag karden pad xēwštan dāštan.nē tuwān,
    awiš dahend juttarīh-ē pad-š nēst.ušān ēdōn abāz abāyēd
    rāyēnēd čiyōn pahrēzōmandīhātar kamzīyānīhātar.

---

1. BTE. <u>alah</u>. See plate.

Answer 4, cont'd.

7) If the Moslem [akdēn] son remains in his akdēnīh and
    does not give it up within a year, he would have no
    share of the family property. That is, all that proper-
    ty is taken away from him and the procedure would be the
    same as mentioned above. Out of that property which
    has been a Zoroastrian property, if they are able to
    seize the share of that akdēn, by virtue of the "law of
    the primitive men," and keep it in their own
    possession and do not give it to that akdēn, they have
    done a lawful act and their seizure is legal.

8) If it is not possible to do so and to seize the proper-
    ty in one's own favor, then there is no other choice but
    letting him [the akdēn] have it. Therefore, they should
    proceed in a way which would be most prudent and least
    dangerous.

pursišn 5

1) pursišn kū dūdag sālārīh kār čiyōn hast.čiyōn bawēd.ka
   dūdag sālār bawēd.uš čiyōn abāyēd pahikārdan ud az kē
   abāyēd pahikārdan.agar andar sāl dranāy pahikārēd.čiyōn
   bawēd.agar pas az sāl dranāy pahikārēd.dādestān čē.uš
   gumārd-i radān ayāb wehān pad kār abāyēd ayāb nē.agar
   pad bēgānagīh bawēd.uš pad dūdag sālarīh ud rāyēnīdārīh
   rāy.ō kas-ē andar šahr andar[1] nibēsēd.šāyēd ayāb nē.

---

1. BTE. omits, whereas similar cases, the use of <u>andar</u> before a verb,
   are frequently encountered in Pahlavi texts: <u>andar šud</u>, <u>andar pēš</u>
   <u>hilēd</u>, <u>andar dwārest</u>, <u>Ayādigār-i Zarirān</u>,ed. Jamasp Āsāna pp. 1, 1(
   <u>andar būd</u>, <u>andar framūd kardan</u>, <u>ibid.</u> pp. 18, 20; <u>andar raft ēstēd</u>
   DK-7 H.S. Nyberg, <u>A Manual of Pahlavi</u>, (Wiesbaden: Otto Harrassowi~
   1974), II, 44.

Question 5

1) The question is: what is [the responsibility of] a
family guardianship, and how should it be fulfilled when
one becomes a family guardian? How should it be claimed?
From whom should it be claimed? If it is claimed within
a year, what is the procedure? If claimed after a year,
what would be the judicial decree? Would a nomination
by the leaders and eminents of the religion suffice
or not? If the appointee is away, and he writes to someone in the city for family guardianship and leadership,
is it permitted?

passox 5

2) agar-š čiš andar nēst ān rāy juttar.dūdag sālarīh sē
   ēwēnag bawēd.kardag, būdag, gumārdag.

3) ān-i kardag ān bawēd kadag xwadāy.andar xwēš zindagīh
   sālārīh-i dūdag i hudādestān awiš kunēd.uš dūdag
   sālārīh kardagīhā.

4) ēwāz[1] mard-ē ōšyār-i pānzdah sālag.pad sālārīh šāyēd.
   pad pusarīh padīrēd.enyā pad pašn-i xwēš gīrēd.

5) ud ān-i būdag ān ka kadag xwadāy az āwām be šawēd.ēg-š
   pus-i tanīgzād-i ōšyār-i pānzdah sālag hast.im pus dūda
   sālārīh būdagīhā.

---

1. Ank. reads ayûp .

Answer 5

2) If there is nothing else implied in this question
which would require another answer, there are three kinds
of family guardianship:[1]   the provided, the existent and
the appointed.[2]

3) The provided type is the one in which the paterfamilias
in his lifetime appoints some one properly according to
the law to be the guardian of his family. This is
called the provided family guardianship.

4) Only a mentally sound male member of the family who has
reached the age of fifteen and who may be eligible for
family guardianship, would receive [the title] either
because of his affiliation [sonship] or through personal
consent.

5) The existent type is that in which, when the paterfamilias passes away, then his kindred son who is sane and
has reached the age of fifteen is chosen as the family
guardian. This son is [called] existent family guardian.

---

1.   "Guardian" is used here for the Pahlavi dūdagsālār , a term including, 1) status as head of the family, 2) the power to make decisions
for and in the name of the absent paterfamilias, analogous to the
powers of an executor.

2.   This classification is reflected in Dādestān-i Dēnīg, chap. 58.

passox 5, cont'd.

6) ān-i gumārdag ān i frāz az widarišnīh-i kadag xwadāy
pad dūdag sālarīh sazāgtar.ud uš āwām sālārān gumārēnd.
uš dādestān gumārdagīhā.

7) dūdag sālārīh pad ān zamān bawēd ka mard-ē i weh dēn
az gētīg bē šawēd.zan ud frazand aburnāyag ud ātaxš-i
wahrām pad dūdag.ka-iz ēk az ēn sē hast.ēg-iz ōh abāyēd
uš brād-i hambāz ud pus-i burnāy ud dūdag sālār ud
stūr-i kardag ud pus-i padīraftag nēst.ēg-š kas-ē.
sazāgtar.pad dūdag sālārīh be gumārišn.

8) ōy pad dūdag sālārīh sazāgtar kē ō ōy i widardag nazdīk
paywandtar.

9) hamē ōy i nabānazdištar pad dūdagsālārīh ōy i widardag
pahikāridan xwāstan frēzbānīg.

10) ka rad ayāb mowbed ayāb dastwar mad ēstēd.ēg-š
pahikārišnīh pad xwāhišn stānišnīh dūdag sālārīh ō ēk
az-išān kunišn.gumārdan-i pad dūdag sālārīh az-š xwāhišn
stānišn.

Answer 5, cont'd.

6) The appointed type is the one in which, after the
   passing away of the paterfamilias, he who is most
   suitable [would be chosen]. He has to be nominated by
   the authorities of the time. His legal status would be
   [called] appointed.

7) The family guardianship is needed when a Zoroastrian
   believer who has a wife, an underaged child, and the
   sacred fire in his household passes away. In the case
   of either of these three, the nomination of a family
   guardian is necessary. If the deceased had no associate-
   brother, or a matured son, or a family guardian, or a
   provided proxy, or a fostered son, then it is necessary
   to nominate a person who is most eligible for his family
   as a family guardian.

8) He who has closest family relationship to the deceased
   is the most eligible for guardianship.

9) It is always obligatory that the deceased's next of kin
   claim the family guardianship.

10) If a religious authority or a priest or a minister is
    present [i.e., the presence of these religious eminents
    is required for the nomination of a guardian], in that
    case his [the nominee's] request to take family guardian-
    ship should be made to one of them.

passox 5, cont'd.

11) agar rad mowbed dastwar ēk-iz nē mad ēstēd.ātaxš-i
    wahrām pad šahr nazdīkīh hast. ēn pahikārišn ōy ātaxš
    madār-i ān ātaxš kunišn.

12) agar-iz ān nēst ud mard-i āsrōn hāwišt pēšag hast.kē
    dādestān āgāhīhā tohm hast.ō ōy pahikārišn.

13) agar ān-iz nē mad ēstēd.ō mard-ē wehdēn.i andar šahr
    ud gyāg meh ud čašmagtar ud husrowtar ud pad ruwān
    dōstīh ud šnāxtārīh paydāgtar.ō ōy pahikārišn.

Answer 5, cont'd.

11) If neither an authority of the religion nor a priest
nor a minister be present, [but] a sacred fire be in
the vicinity, in the town, this claim should be announced
by a regular visitor to that fire.

12) If that situation does not prevail either, a righteous
man who is a student of a priest, whose knowledge of the
religion is rooted in his lineage, to him the request
[of the official declaration of the guardian] should be
made.

13) If that is not available too, any adherent of Zoroastrianism
in that town who is elderly, well known, and with good
reputation, and his veneration for the soul and his wisdom are attested more [than the others'], to him the request [of the official declaration of the guardian] should
be made.

passox 5, cont'd.

14) ka čiyōn mad ēstēd ud pahikārišn kardan gumardan-i[1]
dudagsālārīh pad ān i mad ēstēd.čiyōn weh šāyēd.
awestwārān pad gumārdan nāmag setānēnd.ēg-š mādagwartar
xwēškārīh-ē kū rāyēnīdārīh-i kār-i dūdag pad dūdag
sūdōmandīhātar ud wehdēn dādestānīhātar.kardan
rāyēnīdan.ud tuwān sāmānīhā kār-i dūdag ēdōn rāyēnīdan.
čiyōn ka kadag xwadāy zīndag būd.ēg-š kār-i zan ud
aburnāyag-i andar dūdag ōy ōwōn rāyēnišn čiyōn ān-i
xwad frāztar.

15) ud ka im dūdagsālārīh dēnigīhā[2] ud xūb rāyēnēd ēg-š.az
xwāstag andar īm dūdag hast.pad mizd-i dūdagsālārīh
sīnag-masāy ud bāzā-masāy ud wastarag-ē[3] wahāg rāy.har
rōzag šabān-ē.sē panj ēk-i drahm-ē pad[4] xwēšēnēd.

16) uš kirbag-iz i az xūb rāyēnīdārīh frazandān-i andar
dūdag.parwarišnīh-i ačār[5].ōh bawēd.

---

1. Not in BTE., nor in the MS.

2. BTF. ‏بوایں‎ ‏کرو‎. Ank. reads sūkīhā with a question mark. Men. must
have read it sūdīhā; because in his Feux et Fondations pieuses dans
droit Sassanide, (Paris, 1964), p. 38, he has translated it "profitab
ment", also with a question mark. I think it might be a corrupted
form of ‏بوایںجو‎ dēnīgīhā, or the scribe might have had
dādestānīhā in mind, both of which would mean "lawfully, legally".
See plate.

3. BTF. ‏ادمصر‎(‏وس‎/. Ank. reads vastargīn, which does not seem appro
ate. It might be mis-script of ‏ادمصارو ۳۳‎

4. Ibid. ‏وسل‎. Men. op.cit., p. 38, translates "parfait". Ank. has
read pūr. I think it is corrupted form of ‏ولو‎.

5. Ibid. Ank. amends to aburnāig.

Answer 5, cont'd.

14) When the procedure has been enacted and the act of
claiming and nomination is performed, then it is required that it should be officially recorded by the
religious authorities in written form. From that moment
on, his [the nominee's] prime responsibility would be to
administer his family affairs within the limits of his
power for the most benefit for the family, under the
strictest conformity with the religious law just as when
the master of the house was alive. Thus the affairs
[concerning] the wife and children of the family should
be administered as his most important concern.

15) If he administers his family guardianship lawfully and
properly, then he can take from the wealth of the family
an amount sufficient[1] for his salary and [also] for
clothing expenses [which would come out] about 3/5 of a
drahm[2] per day.

16) To him also would belong the spiritual reward for his
proper upbringing of the children, and nurturing [them]
inevitably is his duty [as well].

---

1. The Pahlavi sinag-masāy, bāzā-masāy, is a translation of Avestic bāzu
stavaghem vā sraoni masanghem: Vd. 6.20, which West has rendered in
the free translation "as much as can be sufficient to make both ends
meet." R.HF. p. 187, note 3.

2. See ans. 3, note 3.

<u>passox 5</u>, cont'd.

17) uš im dūdagsālārīh tā ān hangām pad-š.kadagxwadāy rāy
    pus-ē i ōšyār ō burnāīh rasēd.

18) ka-š pus ō burnāīh mad.im dūdagsālār az dūdagsālarīh
    gohrīg.ud dūdagsālār ān pus bawēd.ēdōn-iz ka dūdagsālār
    xānag.ud ēn-iz kū im čiyōn kadag xwadāy az$^\text{I}$ frāz rawēd.

19) ōy kē pad dūdagsālārišn sazāgtar.ka pad im gyāg mad
    ēstēd.uš pad sālārīh-i dūdag pahikārdan tuwān.ēg-š
    zamānīg pad dūdagsālārīh be pahikārišn.

20) ka-š pahikārdan.tuwān.nē pahikārēd.gumard pad-š nē
    stānēd ēg-š zamānig tanāpuhl wināh, ud zyān-iz i andar
    dūdag bawēd.ēg-š ō bun.

21) ka.pad im ēwēnag. az-š sāl dranāy pad-š widarēd.abar
    dūdagsālārīh ne pahikārēd.gumārd pad-š nē stānēd.uš
    bōzišn bōzagīhā ud čimōmandīhā nēst.pas az sāl dranāy.
    andar dūdag ē margarzān.uš dūdagsālārīh ačār.ud ō ōy
    kas rawēd kē.pas az ōy.ān nabānazdištar ud sazāgtar.

---

1. Ank. amends to _ʊʊ_

Answer 5, cont'd.

17) This family guardianship continues until a sane son of
the paterfamilias reaches maturity.

18) When the son reaches maturity, this family guardian
becomes substituted by this son, who becomes the family
guardian; likewise, the lordship of the house [becomes
his duty], identical with the family lordship of the
paterfamilias prior to his passing away.

19) He who is most eligible, when he reaches the stage and
is eligible to claim guardianship, then immediately he
should do so.

20) If he is eligible for the claim and does not claim, and
does not take the office, then at that very moment he
has committed a tanāpuhl sin. Therefore any harm be-
falling the family would affect his soul.

21) If a year passes like this and he does not claim the
responsibility of family guardianship and does not accept
the selection and his apologies are not contrite and
mournful, then his sin to the family is [considered]
margarzān, and he would become exempted from family guardianship and it would go to the person who is the next
nearest blood kin and the most worthy one.

passox 5, cont'd.

22) ōy.ka awiš mad. dādestān ham čiyōn ān i pēš rāy nibišt.

23) ka sāl dranāy.pad ān ēwēnag.be rawēd.pas az sāl dranāy. ān-iz i pas dādestān čiyōn ān-i pēš. ud pas az ōy.ō ōy rawēd kē.pas az ān nabāzištar ud sazāgtar.

24) agar.pas az be widarišnīh-i kadag xwadāy.pēš kū kas i sazāg pad dūdagsālārīh gumārd.ud gumārd setānēd. dūdag kadagbānūg gādār-ē frāz girēd. padixšā.

25) ka dūdagsālār nē gumārd.dūdag kadag bānūg gādār be frāz girēd.dūdagsālārīh pad gādār be hilišn.

26) dūdag kadagbānūg gādār griftan pad āgāhīhā ud dānišn-i āwām sālārān hast.ka ōh girēd.

Answer 5, cont'd.

22) When the office comes to him [the next in line], the
    conditions are the same as those mentioned above.

23) [In the case of this second nominee] If similarly a
    year passes away the conditions would be identical with
    the above mentioned one. Thus, after him the office
    should be passed over to the person who is the next
    nearest blood kin and more eligible.

24) When a paterfamilias passes away, before a worthy per-
    son is nominated for the office of family guardianship,
    and until the time that such a person accepts his respon-
    sibility, if the lady of the family takes a lover,[1] [it
    is] lawful.

25) If the family guardian is not yet nominated and meanwhile
    the lady of the family has taken a lover, the office of
    family guardianship should be assigned to the lover.

26) Thus, taking of the lover by the lady of the family is
    done with knowledge and awareness of the authorities of
    the time.

---

1. There are some philological problems in interpreting this term.
    See appendix, below.

39

27. dūdagsālārīh kardag.ān-iz i gumārdag.ka dūdagsālārīh
     nē xūb rāyēnēd.ud pad xwāstag ē sē stīr andar dūdag
     hamē nigerišnīgīhā zyān kunēd.ēg-š dūdagsālārīh ačār
     ō bawēd.

28. ān-i kardag.ka be tōzēd.ā-š dūdagsālārīh abāz rasēd.

29. ān-i gumārdag ka be tōzēd.ēg-š gumārdagīh andar abāyēd
     abāz gumārišn.

30. agar ōy.kē pad dūdagsālārīh sazāg.pad bēgānagīh bawēd.
     ka-š āgāhīh rasēd.ānōh kū pad bēgānagīh.raft.rad dastw
     ayāb abārīg i čiyōn abar nibišt hast.ka be pahikārēd.
     wisp[1] i pad pahikārišn i-š rad ayāb ōy kē ānōh mad ēst
     pad dūdagsālārīh pad-š be setānēd.tā pad bēgānagīh.
     ka-š xwad ō dūdagsālārīh āmadan tuwān.ō kas.awestwārīh
     sazēd.nibēsēd.kū-š pad abāyīstīh im dūdagsālārīh rāyēn
     ud ōy.kē awiš tā ka-š nibēsēd.hamgōnag rāyēnīdan padīr
     ud kunēd.šāyēd xūb.

---

1.   BTF. replaces with <u>ud</u>. See plate.

Answer 5, cont'd.

27) As for the "provided" family guardianship, it is similar to that of the "appointed". In case he [the provided] does not fulfill the office properly and manifestly causes a loss of [even] three stir in the family, then he is no longer eligible for family guardianship.

28) In the case of the provided one, if he atones for what he has done, then the office goes back to him.

29) As for the "appointed" one, if he atones, and his re-appointment seems proper, then all the formalities of the appointment should be again performed.

30) If he who is eligible for family guardianship is in another town, on receiving due notice, he should go to a priest or to a minister or to any other [authorities of that town] as mentioned above, and claim according to all formalities of claiming, through a priest or any one else who is present there. Thus he obtains the office. While he is still in that foreign town if he finds himself eligible for the office, confirmability requires that he should write [to someone] that as it is necessary [he] will accept the administration of the family guardianship. In the meantime him to whom he [the future family guardian] has written should [temporarily] undertake and perform the administration. That would be proper.

Appendix

ﺟﺩﺍﺭ MK. gādār, translates as "husband", but for the infinitive gives the Aramaic *ﺷﺩﺩﺗﻭﻥ*, "to copulate". Men. in his <u>Feu et Fondation</u>, p.39, translates "si la maitresse de la maison prend un mari (gādār) c'est licite", but in the same page, note 5, explains that: "Le mot employé n'est pas le terme ordinaire qui designe l'époux (šōy) mais un terme apparement plus grossier, à en juger d'après l'idéogramme sémitique qui le note, pouvant aussi bien désigner l'amant".

The application of such a term in a judicial discussion is noteworthy. In all available Pahlavi[1] references at my disposal, the word *ﺩﺍﺗﺍﺭ* is read dātār with the conventional significances: creator, giver, producer. But when it is the question of cohabitation or copulation, the Aramaic *ﺷﺩﺩﺗﻭﻥ* is used, either in the infinitive or imperative form 2nd.sg. It is only in Mk. that the noun of agency is used. However, the point is that the non-ideogram form is used in this text and, certainly, "husband" is not meant. In Vd. 18,61[2] Zarathusht asked Ahura Mazdā "Who grieves thee with the sorest grief?" Ahura Mazdā answered, "It is the <u>jeh</u> who goes a-whoring after the faithful and the unfaithful, after the worshipper of Mazdā and the worshipper of the Daēvas, after the wicked and the righteous". In the same chapter, sec. 62, note 2, it is

---

1. H.S. Nyberg. <u>Manual of Pahlavi</u>. Abrahamian, <u>Pahlavi Dictionary</u>. Junker, <u>Farhang-i Pahlavi</u>. Harlez, <u>Pahlavi Grammar</u>. Salemann, <u>Pahlav Grammar</u>. Faravashi, <u>Farhang-i Pahlavi</u>. J. Mashkoor, <u>Pahlavi Huzvāris Dicitionary</u>. Dhabhār, <u>Glossary of Pahlavi Yasna</u>. Kāpādia, <u>Glossary of Pahlavi Vendidād</u>.

2. <u>SBE</u>. vol. IV, transl. Darmesteter.

commented that "Whether she gives up her body to the faithful or to the unfaithful there is no difference; when she
has been with three men she is guilty of death." It is am-
biguous whether less than three men is allowed or not. In
R.HF. p. 208, the question is asked of Kama Bohra and Kaus Kama
(both High Priests) "If a man sees another man with his wife
for an illicit deed, what is the decision?" The answer is
"Every woman who gives her body unlawfully to another man four
times, is regarded as jeh. She should be forced to repent
of it and in order that she may desist from doing such misdeeds,
the husband should keep her under his control so that she
cannot persistently do further misdeeds." In Sd.B. Chap. 14,
R.H F. p. 514, it is mentioned that "A woman who consigns her
body to two men in one month is called rūspi (i.e., courtesan)
in the religion, and any woman who consigns her body to two men
in one day is called jeh (i.e. whore) in the religion." The
reason for referring to these few Avestic and Middle Persian
references was to justify the speculation of De Menasce that
the word gādār might mean lover since neither jeh or rūspi is
applicable to the lady of the house. Moreover the two other
terms specifically denote submission of a woman's body to
another man as a matter of lust. But the use of gādār perhaps
conveys the conception that under circumstances a woman is
allowed to have one lover. This rule suggests a society un-
usually tolerant of the rights and interests of women, even

43

by the standards of the present day. There is also another

reference to the same word with the same sense of lover.

See ans. 31, sec. 12, 13, 14, also ans. 42, sec. 4. Inter-

estingly enough, according to these passages there is a legal

term for such a woman [i.e. who takes a lover] bayaspān or

 xwadrāy woman which is entirely different from jēh or rūspi

See R.HF. p. 200, also A. Perikhanian, "On Some Pahlavi Leg

Terms", Henning Mem. Vol. (London 1970), p. 351.

pursišn 6

1. pursišn ēn kū.pad dūdagsālārīh kē sazāgtar.ud kē abāyēd
   gumārdan.agar andar im gyāg rad ud dastwar nē bawēd.
   dādestān čē ud čiyōn.

passox 6

2. pad dūdagsālārīh ōy sazāgtar nazdīk paywandtar ud ōšyār.
   ōy pad-š abāyēd gumārdan.

3. ka rad dastwar nē mad ēstēd.čiyōn azabar.andar dar-i
   pēš az ēn.kē hast ān-i panjōmdar.kunišn.

Question 6

1. The question is: who would be more eligible for family
   guardianship and who should be assigned to it? If there
   is no religious authority or a priest available, what
   would be the situation according to the religious jurisprudence?

Answer 6

2. He who has the nearest lineage and is sane would be
   eligible for family guardianship.

3. If a religious authority or a priest is not available,
   what was written above, in the fifth chapter, should be
   carried out.

pursišn 7

1. mard-i kē-š zañ-ē i pādixšā bawēd.mard widarān bawēd.ud
   pad handarz nāmag gōwēd.kū ēn zan az zanīh ud stūrīh
   man abēzār.az ān xwāstag kē-š bē ō pādixšāīhā-i im mard
   burd būd.abāg im zan dādan frāmōšēd.[1]

2. im mard. čiyōn ān-i azabar nibišt.wināh-ē ō bun bawēd
   ayāb nē.

3. ud agar zan.pas az be widarišnīh-i mard. gōwēd.kū-m.nē
   dānist ku.pad handarz nāmag čē nibišt ēstēd.agar sālārīh
   abāz nē padīrēd.ud az sālārīh-i im mard bē nē ēstēd.ēg-š
   pādixšā bawēd ayāb nē.

4. ud agar mard.pad andarz nāmag.bahr -ē az xwāstag-i xwēš.
   pad ahlawdād.be kas-ē dahēd.zan agar čagar.bawēd čiš-iz
   duš-pahikārišnīh pad-š kardan šāyēd ayāb nē.

---

1. Ank. reads framāyed. See plate.

Question 7

1. If a dying man whose wife is a pādixšā wife, speci-
   fies in his will that "This woman is exempted from being
   my wife and being my proxy", but forgets to point out
   that the property which she had brought to him as a
   pādixšā wife. should be returned to her [from the total
   sum of the property],

2. Under above mentioned circumstances, has this man committed a sin which would afflict his soul or not?

3. If this woman, after the passing away of the man, says,
   "I did not know what was written in the will", and does
   not agree to withdraw from guardianship, would she still
   remain a pādixšā wife or not?

4. And if the man in his will had dedicated a portion of
   his property to someone else by way of charity,[1] and if
   the wife is a čagar, should she be treated in an inferi-
   or manner?

---

1. ahlawdād, pronounced by present High Priests and Parsees of India
   as "ašodāt" is a stipend either in cash or kind given by people
   to the priest to support him financially so that he can perform religious ceremonies and duties for the community without being obliged
   to do other jobs in order to earn money for supporting his family.
   (Similar to Moslem khoms and zakāt. Tr.'s note.).

48

5. agar-š čiš andar nēst ān rāy juttar.az ān čiyōn.

abēzārīh-i zan pādixšāīhä.ud az šōy pādixšāīhā.bē pad

hamdādestānīh-i har dō.ayāb az im zan winähkārīhā-ē

i ēwarīgīhā paydāgīhēd.i šōy.abē hamdādestānīh-i

ziyānag.az zanīh be hištan.padixšā.čiyōn hištan-i[1]jēhīh.

ayāb jādūgīh.ayāb aburdframānih i pad ān i-š frēzwānīg

kardan.ayāb tan az ham wastargīh šōy-i xwēš winähkārīhā

abāz dāštan.daštānmāh abāg wizārdan nē hištan.ayāb pad

daštān ō stūrīh-i šōy šudan.ayāb daštān nihān kardan.

ud tan ō any mard dādan.ayāb-š any winäh i margarzān

jastan.ayāb pad any winäh paydāg būdan.kē wizend-i tan

ud ruwān az-š šāyēd būdan.enyā mard apādixšāīhā[2] zan-i

xwēš abēhamdādestānīh i ziyānag az zanīh be hištan nē

pādixšā.ud ka-š pad abārīg winäh-kārīh-ē i čiyōn

abarnibišt.i ēwarīhā.az zanīh hēlēd[3] gowēd.ziyānag pad-š

nē hunsand.ud hēlēd[4] ō xwēš nē padīrēd pādixšā.

6. ud pad gōwišnīh.mard zan az zanīh-i im mard hilēd.nē

bawēd.ka-š awinähīhā ud akāmagīhā az zanīh hilēd.ka-š

ziyānag pad-š hunsand.ēg-š winäh bawēd pāyag tanāpuhl.

---

1. BTE. omits.

2. Ibid. padēxšāīhā.

3. Ibid. hīštan.

4. Ibid. hištan.

Answer 7

5. If there is nothing else implied in this question which would require another answer, the question is whether divorcing a woman is lawful if it is accomplished by the act of the husband or by agreement of both. [The answer is] Divorcing a woman because of her attested sin, without her consent is lawful, just as the case would be with a whore or a sorcerer or a disobedient who should be duly treated likewise. [Also it would be the same with a woman who] sinfully abstains from copulating with her husband, does not abstain from intercourse during her menstrual period, or while still in menstruation, goes through the procedure of the <u>stūrīh</u> of a husband, or she who hides her mensturation, or she who gives her body to another man, or she who commits any deliberate sin which would afflict the body and soul. On the other hand, if a man undeservedly divorces his wife without the agreement of the wife, it is not lawful. But if on the basis of any of the above-mentioned deliberate sins, he divorces her and says that he is not pleased with her and he does not wish to keep her any longer, that would be legal.

6. For example, if a man divorces his wife despite her dissatisfaction and unwillingness, and the wife is happy with him, then his sin equals <u>tanāpuhl</u>.

passox 7, cont'd.

7. ka-iz zindag.ayāb ka-iz frāz az šōy.ziyānag pad hilištārih
    ham dādestān nē bawēd.ēg-š dādestān ēn kū pad padixšāīhā
    zanīh-i im mard ēstēd.

8. xwāstag i andar dārišnīh-i ziyānag.bē agar andar nigēxta*
    pad zanīh any.pašn ud hastišn abar xwāstag-ē kard ēstēd
    ān rāy juttar.enyā-š pad dūdag-i šōy i pādixšaīhā dārīšn

9. ud agar-š xwarišn dārīšn nihuft paymōxt.andčand-š pāyag
    passazagīhā abāyišnīg.uš andar āyēd xūb.uš ōh kunišn.uš
    ō any hištan šōy rāh nēst.agar wēš.az-š ne setānišn.če-
    šōy be awiš dādan framūd.ud agar kam hišt i-š šōy bunīg
    kunišn.

10. ud agar-iz-š.pad ahlawdād.ō any kas dād ēstēd.uš andčan
    bunīgīh uzēnag-i im zan rāy abāyišnīg.abāz dārišn.ud
    xwarišn ud dārišn-i zan i pādixšāīhā bunīg kunišn.

---

1. See tr. same, note.

Answer 7, cont'd.

7. If [the husband is] alive or after his passing away,
    the wife does not agree to [such] unjust divorce, then
    the law advocates that she should remain as pādixšā
    wife.

8. As for the property in the possession of the wife; if in
    the declaration[1] of her marriage other promises or con-
    tracts regarding the property have been made, the case
    would be different; otherwise legally, it should remain
    in the possession of the husband's family.

9. If she conceals food, provisions, clothing, it would be
    proper to give her as much as she deserves. Such should
    be done.
    If more, it should not be taken from her, because the
    husband has given it to her. But if less, that would be
    encumbant on the husband's soul.

10. If some portion is given by way of ahlawdād, the entire
    expenses of the wife should be taken [from what is left].
    Provision of food and maintenance for a lawful wife is
    a prime responsibility.

اولعدد/۱۱ Ank. is doubtful in reading. The same expression
has occurred in ans. I, sec. 4, also with doubtful reading by Ank.
I think both instances are mis-script of either ۱۱عودپ nigēxtan or
اولوردپ/۱۱ negizišn, meaning to disclose, to expose.

52

passox 7, cont'd.

11.   ud agar zan-ē čagar.ēg-š.frāz az xwēš.pad abēčarīh i
      zan i čagar.uš gōwišn-ē nē hamē abāyēd.če-š xwād az-š
      abēčār.

12.   bē agar-šān pašn-ē ud astišn-ē mayān hast.ēg-š zan-i
      čagar.ka šōy čagar az awām šud.ēg-š sālārīh pad
      pahikārišn-i ō xwāstag az hilišn-i šōy čagar nēst.nē-iz
      ō xwarišn ud dārišn-i az hištan-i šōy čagar nēst.nē-iz
      ō xwarišn ud dārišn az hištan-i šōy čagar.

53

Answer 7, cont'd.

11. If a woman is a čagar , she is already helpless because
    of her being a čagar . Therefore it should not be
    repeated to her face, for she is sufficiently defenseless.

12. Unless there has been especial promise or deal between
    them, a čagar wife, when her husband passes away, has
    no right to claim the property, nor food or provision
    from what her husband has left.

54

pursišn 8

1. mard-ē.kē gowēd.kū.stūr-i man mard mā gumārēd.ēg-š
   wināh ō bun bawēd ayāb nē? agar-š bawēd.čand bawēd?

passox 8

2. mard ka ān-i čiyōn abarnibišt gowēd.hamgōnag gōwišn rāy.
   ēg-š wināh-ē ō bun nē bawēd.bē-š ān-iz kirbag i pad
   pusarīh stūr kunišnīh ud gumārišnīh ud nāmgānīh i pad
   gētīg awiš ne rasēd.

3. čē mard kā-š frazand-i tanīgzād nēst.az kas pad pusarīh
   padīrēd.

4. ud stūr ud nāmgānīh i pad gētīg hištan wuzurg sūd-i tan
   ud ruwān.

5. ēd-rāy.andar weh dēn.kār-i pus-i padīraftag ud stūr ōwōn
   saxt guft ēstēd. ōwōn kū.ka xwad. kas nē paydāgīnēd ēg-š stūr
   be gumārišn.

Question 8

1. If a man says that he does not want any proxy to be
   assigned after him, has he committed a sin afflicting
   his soul or not? If so to what degree?

Answer 8

2. If a man makes the above statement, he does not neces-
   sarily commit a sin afflicting his soul by saying it, but
   he deprives himself of the worldly merits that would en-
   sue from his appointing a proxy, a guardian or one who
   could carry on the family's name.

3. That is why a man who has no blood issue adopts someone
   for his sonship.

4. To appoint a proxy and to try to maintain the family's
   name in the world is of great merit for the body and
   the soul.

5. That is why in Zoroastrian religion the question of
   adopting a son and proxy is so much emphasized. To the extent that if someone does not undertake it himself, a proxy
   should be assigned for him.

pursišn 9

1. mard-ē i hērbed.kē pad drujīh i wināh kārīh kē-š xwad. pad-š hust[1] xwāhēd.

2. radān dastwarān wizīr pad tōzišn pad-š kard.

3. uš tōzišn nē kard.az im wināh be nē wašt.

4. pad yoǰdahrgarīh ud hērbedīh šayēd ayāb nē.

---

1. BTE. ╒ﻢﻌ Ank. reads, <u>an-astub bahot</u>, but mentions in the MS. ﻢﻌ K.J., "Ēmēt i Ašavahistān", <u>Monumentum H.S. Nyberg</u>, (Acta Iranica, Brill, Leiden, 1975), pp. 435-reads <u>hust xwāhad</u>, and in his translation, p. 436, <u>op</u>.<u>cit</u>., note gives his reason for this reading.

Question 9

1. [Suppose] a man who is a teacher-priest[1], by means of false statement, [which is] sinful on his part, demands a parish[2] for himself.

2. The religious authorities and high-priests decide on his atonement.

3. He does not atone and does not revert from the sin.

4. Is he eligible for the office of purifier and priesthood or not?

---

1. Hērbed.

2. It is necessary that every fifteen years, the Hērbeds should divide their dioceses among themselves by casting lots and should receive the jurisdiction of their diocese (pah. ܪܘܣܦ or ܪܘܢ ܪ) in proportion to their Hērbedship and receive the profit therefrom. R.D.BZ. in R.HF., p. 421. [The rank and the income of the hērbed seems to be proportional to the size of the diocese].

passox 9

5. agar-š čiš andar nēst ān rāy juttar.kār hērbedīh
    yojdahrgarīh hast dō kār i mādīg.

6. ēn-iz dō nām-i abēzag dēn āgāhān i rāst gōwišnān šān
    hamēšag handēsēd.[1]

7. mard pad ēn ēwēnag ēg-š pad ēč gōnag nām-iz hērbedīh
    yojdahrgarīh pad-š nē sazāg.uš gōr ud mar-i druwand ud
    ahlomōg-i anahlaw ud jahīg.i pad im dō kār i mādagwar
    rāyēnīdārīh.bē pad-iz dudīgar kār az uskārišn weh dēn
    nē šāyēd.ka-iz pad-š frahixt.ēg-iz pad im kār awestwār
    nē dārišn.awiš nē framāyišn.pad-iz nīrmad az-š nē
    arzānīg.az hamkārān nidan[2] ud abāz dāštan mahist kirbag.

---

1. BTE. ⟨script⟩ Ank. reads, hū-sahēt. K.J., "Ēmēt i Ašvahištan",
    Monumentum H.S. Nyberg, (Acta Iranica, Brill, Leiden, 1975), pp.
    435-6, reads xvēsihēt. I think it is handēsed which has the simi-
    lar meaning of Ank.'s reading with a more justified reading. See NB
    below.

2. BTE. ⟨script⟩ Ank. amends to ⟨script⟩ and reads vizutan, but
    taking it as the corrupted form of heterogam ⟨script⟩ , makes
    more sense. K.J., op. cit., p. 436 reads kašitan.

NB. After consulting the MS. I agree with Ank.'s reading, because it is
    clearly written hūsahēd and not that which is reflected in BTE.
    See plate.

Answer 9

5. If there is nothing else implied in this question
    requiring another answer, teacher-priesthood and the
    mastership of the rite of purification are two very
    important statuses.

6. That is why these two holy designations are always
    [highly] considered by the religious authorities of the
    [religion of the] truthful words.

7. A man of such a nature deserves in no way the appella-
    tion of teacher-priest   or that of the master   of
    the purification rite. He is a wild ass, evil scoundrel,
    a sinful heretic, a whore, who is not qualified for the
    administration of these two major tasks. Also he does not
    deserve to be considered for any other religious position
    Even if he is trained for that, he should not be assigned
    to that. He is not even worthy of the [priestly] share.
    To lead and keep him away from the college would be
    the greatest meritorious deed.

pursišn 10

1. mard-ē.kē hērbed yojdahrgar hast.ō kārezār duzān
    dušmenān šawēd.

2. ēg-š abāyēd šud ayāb nē.

3. agar griftār bawēd.uš dāg ud drōš abar nihēnd.ud
    ka-šān dāg sē abar nihād būd.ēg-š ō dušmenān guft.
    kū.agar pad sē nē hamdādestān hēd.ēk-ē dudīgar abar
    nīhēd.ušān čāhār abar nihād hē.

4. im mard.pad im dar.čiyōn hast.uš xwēškārīh būd.šudan
    ayāb nē.ud kār-i hērbedīh ud yōjdahrgarīh šāyēd ayāb nē

Question 10

1. A man who is a teacher-priest and a master of the purification rite, goes to the battle-field to fight against outlaws and enemies.

2. That being so, ought he to go or not?

3. Suppose him to have been captured. They would have branded him and scarred him. [Suppose] while they were laying three brands on him he were to tell them, "If three does not suffice you put on another." They would have done so and would have laid on four.

4. In what way, would the case of this man be treated in this chapter? Would his going to the battle-field be considered a virtue or not? Would he be eligible to be a teacher-priest or a master of purification rite or not?

passox 10

5. agar-š čiš andar nēst ān rāy juttar.mard kē pēšag
    āsrōīh.nāmčist ān kār hērbedīh ud yōǰdahrgarīh-iz.
    xwēškāmagīh ō kārezār dušmenān šudan axwēškārīha.ud
    har ān wizend ud rēš ud anāgīh.i-š az dušmenān abar
    rasēd.grān wināhīhā ō bun.

6. ud ka xwadkāmagīhā ud axwēškārīhā šawēd.andar šān
    xast griftārihēd.uš anāgīh.pad ēn ēwēnag azabar nibišt
    pad-š kunēnd.ušān abāg-iz stēzēd.aš stēz rāy.drōš wēš
    pad-š kunēnd.ēg-š dādestān azēr bad.čē-š grān wināh
    čiyōn margarzān.i kē-iz nasā ō ātaxš barēd.tan rēman-iz
    pad-š šāyēd būdan.

7. mard.pad ēn ēwēnag.pad kār-i hērbedīh ud yōǰdahrgarīh
    nē šāyēd.ēzišn kunēd ō dēvyazišnīh nazdīk.rēman-iz
    šōstan[1] hil.[2] kū nē yōǰdahrinēd rēmantar be kunēd.

---

1. BTF. šōyēt. So does K.J., "Ēmēt i Ašavahištan", Monumentum H.S.
   Nyberg, (Acta Iranica, Brill, Leiden, 1975), p. 437.
2. Ibid. ‏ او‏ Ank. reads jahik so does K.J. op.cit., p. 437. I
   think the previous word should be left in the infinitive, not
   3rd sg. past as these two scholars have read, and the last word
   is hil, which is another form of hištan. See plate.

Answer 10

5. If there is nothing else implied in this question which
    would require another answer, if a man's career is
    priesthood, in particular the office of teacher priest or
    that of master of purification rite, his going to the
    battle-field wilfully to fight against the enemies is
    not considered a righteous duty. Therefore any harm,
    injury or mischief befalling him from his enemies would
    be a great sin on his part, afflicting his soul.

6. If stubbornly and undutifully he goes and becomes cap-
    tured by them wounded, and they do torture him as men-
    tioned above, and while being tortured, he even argues with
    them, culminating in his being branded more, his case
    would be exceedingly bad. Because his sin is as severe
    as a margarzān, [like] he who carries a dead body to the
    fire, he, [the stubborn hērbed] also has a corrupted
    body.

7. Such a man is not suitable for the office of teacher-
    priesthood or that of the master of purification rite.
    His worship would be like demon worship. He should aban-
    don performing ablution, because not only would he not
    remove any defilement but would cause more pollution.

pursišn 11

1. agar im mard čiyōn ān.az nang.xwēškārīh-i xwēš hilēd.
   ēg-š ō lašgarīgīh ud spāhīgīh šawēd.pad drayāān
   jumbišnīh dīdārag bawēd.

2. agar.pas az ān.abāz āyēd.nē pad rāh-i pašēmānīh-i az
   im[1] kār.pad kār-i hērbedīh ud yōjdahrgarīh šāyēd ayāb
   nē.ud agar.pad pašēmānīh ud tan wīrāstan.pad hamkārīh
   šāyēd ayāb nē.

---

1. K.J. reads _hamkār_ and translates collaborators. "Ēmēt i
   Ašavahištān" _Monumentum H. S. Nyberg_,(Acta Iranica, Brill, Leiden
   1975), p. 438.

Question 11

1. If the afore-mentioned man abandons his duty shame-
   fully, goes to the army and military service, be seen
   crossing the seas,[1]

2. If thereafter,[he] comes back [but] not with repentance
   for what he has done; would he be eligible for the
   office of teacher-priesthood and administration of the
   purification rite or not? and if he repents and re-
   stores his self would he qualify for collegiate responsibility or not?

---

1. Hērbeds are prohibited by the law of religion to travel by sea.
   R.HF. P. 604

passox 11

3.   agar-š čiš andar nēst ān rāy juttar.ēn axwēškārīh.ēg-š
     wināh-iz i margarzān pad-š šāyēd raft būd.

4.   kār-i hērbedīh ud yōǰdahrgarīh dō kār i abēr nāzug.
     nāmčišt kār-i yōǰdahrgarīh.mard-i hū-xēm ud mard-i abēz
     i kamwināh abāyēd kardan.ān i pad wad-xēm i pad-iz
     wināh-i margarzān warōmand nē šāyēd ka kunēd.

5.   mard.ka ēk ǰār.pad wināh i pad ēwēnag i abarnibišt.
     paydāg būd ēstēd.pad im[1] kār ān nē šāyēd.

6.   pas az ān.ka-īz was pašēmānīh ud petītīgīh kunēd.ēg-š
     pad im kār kunišnīh pad ašāyastag dārišn.abāz.ō im kār
     kunišnīh.nē hilišn awiš nē framāyišn.az har dō kār
     akār dārišn.

1.   BTF, ‌جٮس⁩ رٮ . Ank. amends it to ‌جرٮس‌ . K.J., "Ēmēt
     Ašavahištān",Monumentum H.S.Nyberg,(Acta Iranica, Brill, Leiden,
     1975), p. 439, reads hamkārān and translates: He is not fit for
     the (priestly) collaborators. However I believe it makes perfect
     sense to read it as it is (i.e. im kar).

Answer 11

3. If there is nothing else implied which would require another answer, this is (considered) undutiful, for the sin of which the procedure of <u>margarzān</u> should be carried out.

4. The responsibility of teacher-priest as well as that of the master of purification is a very crucial one, in particular that of the purification. A holy man of good character with the least amount of sin should perform it. He who is of low character and susceptible of <u>margarzān</u> sin should not undertake it.

5. A man who has been once proven guilty of the sin, as mentioned above, does not qualify for this job.

6. Even if thereafter he goes through many repentances and penances, he does not deserve the task. He should not be assigned to perform the job. He should be discharged from both responsibilities.

pursišn 12

1. mard-ē hērbed.ka gōwēd.kū.ka yōǰdahrgarīh dānēm.uš
   hamkār pasand-ē ud gumārd-ē abāg nēst.šawēd.mard-ē.
   kē rāy az rēmanīh xwāhēd kū be šōyēd.uš nē xūb šōyēd.
   če-az kēš-i fratom ō abāxtar-rōnag kašēd.nē ō
   <u>rapiθwintar</u> nēmag.uš nē dānist kū-š xūb kard ayāb nē.
   ud ān ka.pas az ān.any kas pad yōǰdahrgarīh ē šōyēd.
   im mard.kē pēš pad ēn hērbed šust būd.dīd.uš guft.kū
   man nē xūb šust hēm.uš ō any mard guft.kū-t nē xūb
   šust hēm.ud im hērbed guft.kū rāst.če-m nē xūb šust
   hē.

2. uš.az nōg.abāz šustan.andar ham gyāg.yōǰdahrgar-ē
   gumardag būd hēnd.

3. pēš az šustan-i ēn hērbed im mard.ud pas-iz hērbed
   dādestān čē.ud pad yazišn-i yazdān šāyēd ayāb nē.

Question 12

1. [Assume that] a h̄erbed claims that he knows [the
    rite of] purification, [but] has not an approved
    or appointed assistant. [Nevertheless] he proceeds
    [with the job]. He tries to wash off the impurities
    of a man, [but] does not wash him properly. Because
    [from the beginning] he draws the first furrow towards
    the north, not towards the south.[1] And he does not
    know whether he has done it correctly or not. And when
    thereafter another man is being washed by a [another]
    master of purification, this [first] man who has been
    washed by the [unskilled] h̄erbed, sees [it] and says,
    "I have not been washed properly". Then he tells the
    other man (i.e. the unskilled h̄erbed), "You did not
    wash me properly". The h̄erbed says, "That is right, I
    did not wash you properly".

2. "You should be washed anew". [So] in the very same
    place, [another] master of purification rite is appointed.

3. What is the law or decision for this h̄erbed before he
    washed this man, and also after that? Is he qualified
    to perform the worshipping rites for the deities[2] or not?

---

1. For details about the rite of washing, which is called barašnum,
    see R.HF., pp. 370-71, also J. Modi, Religious Ceremonies of the
    Parsees, (Bombay, 1922), pp. 102-48.

2. K.J. translated God, "Emet-i Ašavahištān", Monumentum H. S. Nyberg,
    (Acta Iranica, Brill, Leiden, 1975), p.441.

pursišn 12, cont'd.

4. uš tōzišn kardan abāyēd ayāb nē.agarš abāyēd kardan.
    ēn čiyōn abāyēd kardan.

5. agar mard.kē-š šust.rēman bawēd.ēg-š dādestān čiyōn

6. ka-šān az im hērbed pursēd.kū.čē rāy.ka-t nē dānist
    kardan.ēg-t kard.uš pad bōzišn guft.kū.kū-m pad
    dastwarīh wāhmān rad kard. ka wizohišn pad-š kard.im
    rad čiš-iz pad ān ēwēnag nē guft būd.

<u>Question 12</u>, cont'd.

4. Ought he to atone or not? If so, how should it be
   done?

5. If the man he had washed [still] was not clean, what
   would be the applicable religious rule?

6. If they asked this <u>hērbed</u>, "Why did you do that [i.e.
   the performance of purification rite] when you did
   not know? And he, by way of excuse says, "I followed
   the pattern of such and such religious authority". And
   when investigation was made [it turned out] that the
   religious authority had not said anything to that effect.

passox 12

7. agar-š čiš andar nēst.i ān rāy juttar.ka yōǰdahrgar-ē
   pad pasand gumārdag andar šahr ud gyāg būd.im mard.kē
   kār-i yōǰdahrgarīh nē kard ēstēd.abē pasand-i frahixtān
   gumārdag-i dēn dastwarān.kār-i yōǰdahrgarīh kardan
   axwēškārihā bawēd.[1]

8. ān kē nērang ud yōǰdahrgarīh bunīgīhā nē danēd.ēg-š
   yōǰdahrgarīh kardan nē dastwarīhā.ud ka kunēd.grān
   wināhīhā.

9. ud agar-š nērang-i yōǰdahrgarīh āmōxt ēstēd.dānēd kardan
   nē pad nigerišn.bē pad sūdagīh.čiš-ē az-š juttar kunēd
   az ān-i abāyēd kardan.ēg-iz wināh.pad sūdagīh.wināh
   xwārtar.

10. uš tōzišn andar ōy kunišn kē-š šust.

11. ud ka-š im mardōm pad-š hilēd.ahlawdād kunēd.ēg-š wināh
    az bun bē šawēd.

---

1. Ank. amends to būd.

Answer 12

7. If there is nothing else implied which would require
   another answer, had there been an approved and appointed
   master of the rite of purification in that town or in
   that locality, it would have been improper for this man,
   who had not [thus far] performed the rite of purification, to undertake it without the approval of trained
   and appointed religious authorities.

8. He who does not know the rite of the incantation and
   that of the purification thoroughly, but nevertheless
   performs it, his purification is unauthorized, and if
   he does so, [it is a] great sin.

9. And if he has learned the incantation and the purification [rite] and knows how to perform them, and not intentionally, but by negligence, performs something other
   than what he ought to, then [it is considered a] sin of
   negligence, [i.e.] a lesser sin.

10. He shall undergo atonement on the account of the person
    whom he had washed.

11. And when the people forgive him, [and he] gives charity,
    then his sin will be totally removed.

passox 12, cont'd.

12. uš yazišn-i yazdān kardan.uš nē appār.

13. ud ka pas.az xūb nērangīhā.ud rāstīhā.abāz šōyēd.ē
    ka-š im mard ayāb any mard dēn nērangīhā šōyēd.šāyēd.

14. ud ka ān-i rēman nē xūb šōyēd.grāntar kū ān-i kē apāk-
    ihēd. [1] tā ka xūb nērangīhā.pad yōǰdahrgarīh-i xūb
    pasand abāz šōyēd.rēman.har ān wināh i-š andar āb ud
    ātaxš ud zamīg ud abārīg spenāg mēnōg dām az-š rawēd.
    hamāg ān yōǰdahrgar ēdōn ō bun ē bawēd čiyōn kā-š xwēs
    nigerišnīhā kard hē.uš andar ōy kē-š nē xūb šust.wināhkā
    čiš-iz i-š uš abar āxest.warišt [2] i-š abar abganēd.āb-iz
    i-š abar rēxt.ēn hamāg adādīhā.ud kamest sē sad stīr
    ēwkardagīhā bawēd.

---

1. ⟨script⟩ Ank, reads pāk šōyed, so does K.J. in "Eēmēt-i
   Ašavahištān", Monumentum H.S. Nyberg, (Acta Iranica Brill, Leiden,
   1975), p. 440. Since the meaning of this reading is obscure, I
   think it is a mis-script of ⟨script⟩ from a-pāk meaning soile
   and I have translated it accordingly. For the word a-pāk, see Nyberg,
   Manual of Pahlavi, p. 21.

2. For more information about this word, see Vd. 5.51, also H.K. Mirz
   article in J.J, Zarathoshti Madrassa Centenary Vol., Bombay, 1967,
   43, sec. 5., also šāyest lā šāyest, 2-49.

12. Thereafter, he would no longer be barred from [the
    rite of] worshipping the deities.

13. If, afterwards, with proper incantation and due order,
    he washes the same man or any other man, in conformity
    with religious incantations; it is [religiously] per-
    missible.

14. If he does not properly wash the impurities, [his sin
    is] greater than he who has become polluted.[1] And un-
    til he washes [him] again properly, with correct incan-
    tation and conformity with the rites of purification,
    [he will remain] impure. Any sins of his [the person
    who has not been washed properly] which would afflict
    the water, the fire, the earth, or other creation of the
    Bountious Spirit[2] would be counted on the soul of the
    [unskilled] master of purification, as though he himself
    had committed them deliberately. He is guilty regarding
    the man whom he did not wash properly. Any action per-
    formed by him [such as] the ashes[3] he has sprinkled or
    the water which he has poured, all were unlawful. The
    least [punishment of which] is three hundred stīr alto-
    gether.

---

1. See note 1, same ans.

2. Pahlavi spenāg-mēnog. is the creative power of the world as opposed
   to ganāg-mēnog, the destructive power of the world.

3. See same transcription, note 2. [These ashes are taken from the
   Bahrām Fire, the earthly representative of lightning, and the most
   powerful destroyer of fiends.]

passox 12, cont'd.

15. yōǰdahrgar.kē pad nigerišnīh nērang-ē juttar kunēd kū
    ān az weh dēn pad-š paydāg.margarzān.

16. ēn kār-ē hast.pad dānišnīhā ud rāstīhā ud pasand az
    šnāxtārān dastwarān dēn.abāyēd kardan.

17. kē awahāgīhā ud harzagīha kunēd.jēhīg pad yōǰdahrgarīh.
    bē pad-iz yazišn-i yazdān kardan nē šāyēd.

15. A master of purification who intentionally performs
    a ritual other than that which is revealed in the
    Zoroastrian religion, deserves death.

16. This [purification ceremony] is a procedure which ought
    to be carried out with skill, rectitude, and approval
    of the authorities of the religion.

17. He who performs it, not with conformity but loosely,
    [resembles] a jeh with regard to the purification rite.
    Further[more] he is not even suitable to perform [the
    rite of] worshipping the deities.

pursišn 13

1.   šahr-ē kē-š mard i yōǰdahrgar pad-š nē bawēd.uš kas
andar rēman bawēd.uš yoǰdahrgar az any šahr āwurdan nē
tuwān.uš.andar sē hāθra yōǰdahrgar nē bawēd.ēg-š čē
abāyēd kardan.ud dādestān-i mard ud zan pad ēn pursišn
ēk hast ayāb nē.ud ēd kū hāθra čē ud čand paymānag
bawēd.ud meh ud keh bawēd ayāb nē.

Question 13

1. In a city where there is no master of the rite of puri-
    fication and wherein someone is polluted, and it is
    not possible to bring a master of the rite of purifica-
    tion from another town; [also] there is no master of
    purification within three hāθra; under these circum-
    stances what ought to be done? Is the applicable reli-
    gious rule the same for men and women in this case?
    What is a hāθra? What measure does it designate? Is
    it a standard measure? or is it flexible?

passox 13

2.   ōy kē pad any nasā rēman būd ēstēd.ēg-š bowandag
     yōǰdahrgarīh az rēmanīh ēdōn bawēd kū wehdēn
     nērangīhā pad baršnūm šōyēd.

3.   ka yōǰdahrgar.kē pad baršnūm soyēd.andar šahr nēst.uš
     az any šahr ō xwēš āwurdan nē tuwān.xwad ō nazdīk
     yōǰdahrgar-ē barēd.

4.   uš awiš šudan.ayāb-š ō xwēš āwurdan.xwēstan az rēmanīh
     yōǰdahrēnīdan tuwān sāmānīhā čē frēzbānīg.

5.   hāθra.wāz-ē abestāīg.pad ēwāz-i pārsīg frasang xwānēnd.

6.   haθra.meh dwāzdah hazār gām.ud ān i mayānag dah hazār.
     ud ān i keh šaš tā hašt hazār gām bēd.

Answer 13

2. He who has become impure in contact with dead matter, his complete purification from that impurity would only occur when he is washed according to the formali- ties of bar̆snūm[1] in conformity with the rituals of the Zoroastrian religion.

3. If there is no master of purification in that town who would wash him in accordance with bar̆snūm, and [if] he [the master] cannot be brought from another town, then he himself [the polluted] should go to a master of purification.

4. Going to him, or bringing him to one's self, [enabling one's self] to get purified, within one's possibilities from impurities is an obligatory duty.

5. [As for] hāθra; it is an Avestic term. In the dialect of Pars it is called farsang .

6. Hāθra at its most is twelve thousand paces; at its least six to eight thousand paces. Ten thousand paces is the average.

---

1. Ceremonial bath; ritual purification. See R.HF., pp.370-71, also J. Modi, The Religious Ceremonies and Customs of the Parsees, (Bombay, 1922), pp. 97-168.

pursišn 14

1. šahr-ē kēš hērbed dō pad-š hēnd bawēnd.ēk yōǰdahrgar
   ud ēk nē.ušān har dō juddēwdād warm.ud āb dastšōy
   nēst.

2. pad yaštan-i āb ud gōmēz čiyōn abāyēd kardan.

Question 14

1. [Assume] a town in which there are two herbeds; one
of them is the master of the rite of purification, the
other one is not. Both of them know Vendidād[1] by
heart. [But in that town] there is no āb[2] and no
dastšōy.[3]

2. What should be done for the consecration of the water
and the gomēz [i.e. cattle   urine]?

---

1. The word Vendidād comes from the Avestic word vi-daēva-dāta, i.e.
the law given against Daēvās [i.e. evil spirits]. It is that
section of Avesta (the holy book of Zoroastrians) which consists
mainly of explanations of religious rites and duties.

2. "Consecrated water" used for religious rites.

3. dastšoy, a cult term designating the ceremony of ablution with
cattle urine.

passox 14

3. agar-š čiš andar nēst ān rāy juttar.ka-šān har dō gumān
ēd kū pad tan rēmanīh nēst.čiyōn hēnd mad ēstēd.yaštan
ēk abāg did abāz wirāyēnd.ud ōwōn kunēnd i-šān yašt[-i]
wirāst dārišn.ud āb ud dastšōy.weh dēn nērangīhā.be
yazēnd.ud dēn nērangīhā kār framāyēnd.šāyēd.pad hamāg
yōjdahrgarīhā.bē ān-i pad yazišn-i pad sīh gām.čē.
yazišn-i pad sīh gām ēdōn šāyēd kū pad āb ud dastšōy i
pad sīh gām yašt ēstēd.

Answer 14

. If there is nothing else implied in this question which would require another answer, if there is no doubt of physical impurity in the case of either of them as their [the hērbeds] case happens to be, they can arrange for the worshiping[1] ritual between themselves, identical with that of yašt-i wirāst.[2] Then they can consecrate the water and the cattle's urine in conformity with the religious rites. [then] They should recite and perform the religious rites. However, all masters of the rites of purification should respect the principle of thirty steps[3] consecration because the principle of the thirty steps rule should be considered when there is a need to consecrate the water or the cattle's urine.

Pahlavi yaštan has a very wide range of application such as to offer prayers, to worship, to consecrate, to recite religious incantations to revere, to honor.

yašt-i wirāst (yašt-i wirāst) [properly arranged worship] as against yašt-i gumanīg [doubtful worship]) is a yasna ceremony performed by priests for qualifying themselves with the greater Khub and for performing higher liturgical rites. R.FH. pp. 410-415. As for greater Khub, there are two kinds of Khub: greater and smaller. A priest with greater Khub is he who can perform higher liturgical services. For details see J. Modi, Ceremonies of the Parsees (Bombay, 1922), p. 147.

For references of the thirty steps in Avesta, see Vd. 3-17, 7-63, 8-7, Darmesteter's transl., SBE. IV.

86

pursišn 15

1. <u>ham-raēθwa</u>[1].kadār <u>paiti-raēθwa</u>[2].kadār bawēd.

passox 15

2. hamrēd hamkarzagīh-i tan-i mard abāg nasā.ud ayāb
    nasā abāg jāmag[-i] tan-i mard.ayāb jāmag abāg nasā.

3. padrēd ān i ka.mayān-i nasā ud tan-i mard.any-iz čiš
    hast.čiyōn gyānwar.any-iz čiš pad ēd paywand jumbīnēd

---

1. Avestic equivalent for Pahlavi <u>hamrēd</u>.
2. Avestic equivalent for Pahlavi <u>padrēd</u>.

Question 15

1. What is direct defilement? What is indirect defile-
    ment?

Answer 15

2. Direct defilement is the contamination of the body
    of a person with a corpse or the [contact of] dead
    matter with the clothing of a person, or the contact
    of the clothing with dead matter.

3. Indirect defilement is when there is something else
    in between, such as an animal. Also when it is trans-
    mitted by way of another mobile thing [it is considered
    indirect defilement].

88

pursišn 16

1. jāmag-i pambagēn kē-š hixr-i murdagān pad-š bawēd.
ēg-š dādestān čiyōn.

2. pambagēn mōyēn ud pašmēn.har sē ēk ayāb nē.

3. ud agar abāg nasā hamkaržag bawēd.ān gyāg kūš nasā
hamkaržag bawēd.ān gyāg kū-š nasā pad-š abāz ēstēd.
ēwar šnasēd[1] uš az-š burēd.ān-i dudīgar pad kār šāyēd
ayāb nē.

4. uš čiš-iz meh sūdīh pad akār nē kardan hast ayāb nē.

5. ud agar ān jāmag pad pardāxtan-i nasā jumbīnēd.čiš
juttarīh az ān ka nē jumbīnēd hast ayāb nē.

---

1. BTE. ⟨ارسسرم⟩ Ank. amends it to ⟨ارسسرم⟩ and reads snākhta.
K.J. reads šnāyēt, "On Emeīt i Ašavahištan", <u>Cama Oriental Institute Golden Jubilee Vol</u>., (Bombay, 1969), p. 41. See plate.

Question 16

1. What is the applicable religious rule regarding the
    cotton clothes containing the bodily refuse[1] of a dead
    person?

2. Is [the applicable religious rule for the material
    made of] cotton, hair [fur], or wool the same or not?

3. If that cloth is contaminated with dead matter , and the
    spot where the dead matter contacted it is vividly re-
    cognized and is cut from [the rest of] it, would the re-
    maining piece be usable or not?

4. Would there be any greater advantage in not making it
    [the cloth] useless, or not?

5. To shake the cloth in order to remove the dead matter
    from it, would the case be different from that when it
    is not shaken?

---

1.   Pahlavi _hixr_ designates bodily refuse, consisting of bones, flesh,
      skin, blood, pus, hair, nails, semen, genital discharges, and sweat.
      K.J. _op_. _cit_., p. 42.

<u>passox 16</u>

6. wistargīg ud wistarag jāmag-i pambagēn mōyēn ud pašmēn.
   pad rēmanīh-i az hixr ud nasā har sē ēk.

7. ān kē hixr-i murdagān pad-š.ud ō nasā-i murdagān nē
   pahikōft ēstēd.ān and gyāg.kū-š hixr-i murdagān pad-š.
   be burišn.abārīg pāk.

8. ud ān kē-š hixr-i murdagān pad-š.ud ō-iz nasā-i murdagā
   pahikōft ēstēd.ān and gyāg.kū-š hixr-i murdagān pad-š be
   burišn.abārīg pad <u>xšvaš mąnghō</u>[1] <u>šȯ̆yēd</u>.

9. ān-i pad <u>xšvaš mąnghō</u> abāyēd šustan.ka nē pad gōmēz-i
   gāw ēdōn šȯ̆yēd čiyōn andar weh dēn guft ēstēd.pāk nē
   bawēd.

---

1. 𐬱𐬀𐬱 𐬨𐬁𐬵 is Avestic equivalent for Pahlavi
   šaš māh (six months). Vd. 7.15.

Answer 16

6. [The case of] cotton, hair [fur], and woolen bed cloth-
    ing or body clothing which has become contaminated
    through contact with bodily refuse and dead matter, all
    three would be the same.

7. That which has had the bodily refuse of the dead on it
    and has not touched the corpse of a dead person, the
    part which has had bodily refuse on it should be cut
    off, the rest is clean.

8. Of that cloth, which has been in contact with bodily re-
    fuse and carrion, the bodily refuse-contaminated section
    should be cut and the remaining part should be washed in
    conformity with the rite of the "six-months' process".[1]

9. As for that which is necessary to be washed according
    to the "six months' process", if it is not washed by the
    urine of the cow, as specified in the Zoroastrian reli-
    gion, it will not be [considered] clean.

---

1. For details see Vd. 7.15.

passox 16, cont'd.

10. ud har wistargīg jāmag ayāb wistarg-i abāg nasā-i
murdagān hamkaržag bawēd.šustan dastwarīhā.andčand
ēwkardag hamāg rēman.pad x̌svaš mąnghō šuyišn.čiyōn
sarband-ē ka dārišn.ayāb wēš ud kam.and čand hast.
ka-š tēx hambun-iz ō nasā-i murdagān pahikōft hamāg
rēman.ēdōn ān-i čiyōn pērāhan-ē ud kap-ē ud šalwār-e
i dōxtag.ka-š tēx hambun-iz ō nasā-i murdagān pahikōft
hamāg rēman.[1] ēdon-iz šādurwān-ē ud parik-ē ud abārīg-ē
az ēn ēwēnag.ka-š tēx hambun-iz ō nasā-i murdagān pahikč
hamāg rēman.

11. har ān i-š šȯyišn kār.pad x̌svaš mąnghō.šȯyišn.

12. rēmanīh-i jāmag pad hamkarzagīh nē.pad jumbišn pad
hamkaržagīh-i nasā i mardōmān ud sag sardagān ō bawēd.

---

1. The underlined words are missing in the MS. and are supplied by
Ank. in BTE.

Answer 16, cont'd.

10. Washing of any bed clothing or body clothing which has
    become contaminated through dead matters of the dead is
    a religious duty. [No matter] how much it has been in
    contact, the entire part is [considered] contaminated
    and it is necessary to be washed in accordance with the
    "six months' process". The case would be likewise with
    a head scarf if worn. However much or little, even if
    as much as a [needle] point has been in contact with the
    dead matters of a dead, the totality of it is [considered]
    contaminated. The same applies to a sewn dress or hat
    or trousers. Even as much as a [needle]point of contact
    will pollute the whole. The same applies to rugs and
    curtains; or other similar things if even as much as a
    [needle] point is contaminated through the contact of the
    dead matters of a dead body, the whole is considered contaminated.

11. Anything that needs washing [ritual] should be washed
    according to the "six months' process".

12. Contamination of clothing is not [only] through direct
    contact, [but] also by indirect transmission of the corpses
    of men and types of dogs.

94

13. pad-iz ēn rēman ōh bawēd ka mard andar hangām-ē ka pad
     any nasā rēman bawēd.ēg-š wistarg-ē.ayāb wistarīg
     jāmag abāg tan hamkarzag.pad hamkarzagīh rēman bawēd.
     pad xšvaš mąnghō.šoyišn.ān i pad akār dārišn.ud pad akār
     be abganišn.uš šoyišn nēst.pad čiš-iz kār framūdan nē
     dastwarīhā.ka kār framāyēnd grān wināh.

Answer 16, cont'd.

13. Also, contamination may occur at a time when a person,
    while already contaminated by other dead matter, a bed
    clothing or body clothing touches [his] body. This con-
    tact transmits contamination and [the clothing] must be
    washed in conformity with the "six months' process".
    As for not using [the cloth] and discarding it as use-
    less, that which does not fall in the washable category,
    it would not be religiously lawful to use. If it is
    utilized it would be a great sin.

96

pursišn 17

1. puhl-ē.kē abar pad rāh-i rōstag bast ēstēd.abar hušk[1]
rōd-ē.kē hangām bawēd ka widār pad-š kardan.bīm pad
tan xwāstag rāy.nē tuwān.uš pad any hangām pad-š rafta
widardan saxt dušwār.ud ōbastag ud awēran hast.

2. uš uzēnag-i az nōg abāz kardan meh sūdīhātar.ayāb ka
ēn drahm pad any kirbag uzēnag kunēnd.[2]

3. ud agar pad any kirbag meh sūdīhātar.ēn kū ān kirbag
čē hast framāyēd.

4. ēg paydāgēnēd kirbag-i puhl abar rōd-ē nāydāg bastan
čand.

---

1. See appendix, below.

2. Ank. BTE. reads kunēd; so does K.J. "Aspects of Kirpag"
Mémorial Jean De Menasce, (Imprimérie Orientaliste,
Louvain, 1974) p. 240.

Question 17

1. A bridge had been constructed over a dry river-bed[1]
    on a village road. At times it is not crossable for
    fear of [possible accident befalling] people and [their]
    properties, and at times [when one is obliged to] pass
    and cross, it is with great difficulty. It is deteri-
    orating and falling.

2. Would the money spent on reconstructing [this bridge]
    be more rewarding, or that spent on other good deeds?

3. If [spending that money] on other good deeds would be
    more rewarding, could you direct us to the nature of
    those good deeds?

4. [Analogously], explain to us how rewarding would it
    be to construct a bridge over a navigable river?

---

1.   See note 1. of same sec. of transcription.

98

Appendix

: Ank. reads hŭsk; so does K.J. "Aspects of
Kirpag," <u>Mémorial Jean De Menasce</u> (Imprimerie Orientaliste,
Louvain, 1974), p. 240. Despite the agreement of my Iranian
studies professors at Columbia University with the above
reading and its significance as "a dry river bed," I have
my humble suggestion as the following: I believe it is a
corrupted form of ﻫﻮﺗﮓ <u>hutag</u> ("fast running"). Construction of a bridge over a fast running river seems to be a
more urgent need than a bridge over a dry river bed which
at certain times of the year might become impassable. In
Vd. 14-16 there is a reference to certain sin, the atonement
for which is construction of bridges over seven ﺭﻮﺩ rōd
(river). Also in Vd. 18-74 there is another reference to
building bridges over 30 navigable rivers ﻧﺎﻳﺪﺍﮒ nāydāg
as an atonement for an especial sin. These two particular
references are referred to in sec. 26 of our text where it
says: ud ān-i abar wirāstan-i puhl-ē abar ﺭﻮﺩﺍ rōd-ē.pad
māmčist nibišt, meaning: as for the construction of a bridge
over ﺭﻮﺩﺍ river which is mentioned in particular. This
nāmčist (in particular) seems to refer to the cardinal
atonements which are fully treated in <u>Vendidād</u>, amongst
which must be the two above mentioned instances. Considerin
these facts it is difficult to imagine that in this text
which all through is a revision of the most significant

benefactions in Zoroastrian religious laws, the idea of an
exceptional concept might have occurred to Hēmit, i.e.
constructing a bridge over a dry river bed as an obligatory
benefaction. Besides, the letter ⌒𝖴 in the MS. has a clear
angle, different from the other ⌒𝖴 (š) in the same folio,
thus as suggested by Dr. Mirza, the scribe might have been
under the influence of the pronunciation of ⌐ (d) instead
of the letter 𝗉 (t), i.e. dāk instead of tāk as is
pronounced even now by the Parsis. As for the absence of
recurrence of the same word, H. K. Mirza confirms that many
words have been encountered only once in Pahlavi texts.

passox 17

5. agar-š čiš andar nēst ān rāy juttar.saxwan-i pad im

    rāyēnišn drang.uš gōšag-ē ēdar paydāgēnēd payrāst.

    dānāgān uš hangōšīdag kardan.amā pad xwēš xūb xradīh

    ud drust šnāsīh pad-š činaggarīh[1] kardan.čiyōn weh

    wēnēd rawāgēnīdan čimīgkārīhā.

6. ēd dānēd kū kirbag hamē ān mādagwartar i andar hangām

    mādagtar.ud andar ān i mādagtar ān i meh dādestāntar.

    andar ān i meh dādestantar ān i meh sūdtar.andar ān i

    meh dādestantar ān i meh sūdtar.andar ān i wuzurg sūdī

    ān i zamānīg frayādišnīgtar.

7. ud hangird ēn kū pad ōy.kē-š kirbag kāmēd kardan.ān

    sūdīgtar ud weh kū hamē kirbag mad ēstēd ud be šāyēd

    kardan be kunēd.

---

1. BTE. ملعووٮٮٮٮ . Ank. amends to ملبر ٮٮٮٮٮٯ . K.J. ,"Aspect
    of Kirpak" ,Memorial Jean De Menasce, (Louvain. 1974), p. 240, re
    vicēnākgarīh.

Answer 17

5. If there is nothing else implied in this question
    which would require another answer, any comment on
    this matter would take long to formulate. At this
    juncture an aspect [of it] will be pointed out and
    [will be] elaborated. The intelligent ones [are] to
    make analogy. By means of our adequate reasoning and
    right recognitions we have to choose. You should
    apply it usefully.

6. Be aware that the most cardinal benefaction is that
    which is more propitious at a crucial time. And in
    that crucial [time] the more propitious is the one
    which is more lawful, and that which is more lawful
    is the one which is more profitable, and that which is
    more useful for the circumstances.

7. In short, he who desires to do a good deed, the best
    and most profitable [way is that] when the [opportunity
    of doing] good deed arises, and that [deed] should be
    done, he does it.

102

8.   ān rāy nē spōzēd kū ma agar ēn meh weh bawād frāz rasēd

ān kunēd.čē.bawēd kū.spōz rāy.ān i mad ēstēd akard frāz

mānēd.ān i meh ud weh kardan nē rasēd.čē.ān i xwārtar

kirbag.ka kard.ō meh pāyagīh ud meh frayādīh madan

ēmēdwārtar kū ān i wuzurg kirbag kē nē kunīhēd.uš

hambun-iz absīhenīdan kirbag.

9.   ud was ēwēnag sūdīh i az-š nē ētōm.[1] čē hast iš meh

sūdīh andar ēwāzīgīhā.ud hast i amaragānīh.ud hast i

wēš kirbagtar.ud hast i har dō pad-š.ham amaragānīg ud

ham ēwāzīg.

---

1.   See   K.J.,"Aspects of Kirpak", <u>Mémorial Jean De Menasce</u>, (Imprime
Orientaliste, Louvain, 1974), p.245.

. One should not hesitate [to do a good deed] on the account

that [later] a greater and a better one might come up.

This is because there have been instances in which, because

of hesitation, that which could have been accomplished has

remained unaccomplished and that which is greater and better

to perform may never happen. Therefore, a less significant

good deed accomplished promises a better position and sup-

port than that of a greater good deed which is never

achieved, [resulting] even in complete cessation of bene-

faction.

. Various great benefactions are not all the same. There-

fore there are [certain ones] whose benefit is exclusive

and [certain ones] which are general, and there are some

[which are] of more merits and there are some which have

the quality of both; [i.e.] exclusiveness and generality.

passox 17, cont'd.

10. ud ān i amarazānīg wēššūdīh.čiyōn šahristān diz ud

drubuštīh.pad gyāg ēstišnīg sazēd.wirāstan.ātaxš-i

wahram nišāstan.rōd kahas ud jōy az wēš āb ō kam āb

gyāg rāyēnīdan.puhl abar rōd-i nāydag ud abārīg-iz

widārag-i ābān.nāmčist ān-i dušwidārag.bastan.ud

zamīg ud gyāg awērān ābādān kardan.asp zēn ud tōšag

ō ōy kē anērān az wināhišn pad ērānag kardan abāz

dārēd.dādan.ēn ō awestwārān andar abāyēd.ēn hangām kam

dānišnīh rāy.ēn ēwēnag pad pahrēztar abāyēd kardan.

jōrdā abārīg-iz urwar i xwarišnbar kištan.wisigān[1]

pahrēxtan wuzurg kirbag.az ēn hamāg mādagwartar.dūdag

i wehān frarōrān paydāg.kē wadzamānagīh ud asazāg

āwāmīh ēstēd.ayārēnīdan.abāz ō farraxīh ud padēxīh

ud huziwišnīh zāmēnīdan ud abrāzēnidan.ud abartar

ud abērtar ān āsrō pēšagān.andar āsrō pēšagān ān i

abēzag menišn dēn burdārān.ān kē wēš kardārīh ud wēš

dānišnīh pad weh dēn rāy.sazāgīhā ud arzānīgīhā ān i

dēnbedīh ud dastwarīh čimīgīha ud xwēšīg.

---

1. Ank. reads sāyakan. K.J. "Aspects of Kirpak" , Memorial Jean De
    Menasce, (Imprimerie Orientaliste, Louvain, 1974), pp. 241 and 245 r
    sahikan and translates "worthy". See plate. H.K. Mirza suggested
    wēsagān (forest, woods), NP. bēsa.

nswer 17, cont'd.

0. That which is general is more meritorious, such as [building] town fortifications or fortresses on a spot suitable for their standing, establishing the wahrān fire, furnishing river channels, and streams from places with more water supply to those with less water supply, constructing bridges over navigable rivers and other water passages, particularly those of difficult passages, cultivating desolate lands and spots, providing horse equipment and provisions for him who restrains the non-Iranians from doing damage to the Iranians. This is a requisite for the adherents [of Zoroastrianism]. In this era, owing to inadequate knowledge, this custom should be carried out with more reservation. To sow corn as well as other frutiful plants, and to take care of village[1] properties is [considered] a great benefaction. More important than all these is to help, to delight, to lead and to raise to a better life, the descendants of virtuous, righteous and noble families whose excellence and nobility is evident and whom the hardship and unfavourable course of time have brought demerit, suffering and miseries, particularly, and in a higher degree, those descendants from the priestly career; among those of the priestly career, those [who are] holy minded and upholders of the religion, who in respect of more activity and more knowledge of the religion are fit for and deserve religious leadership and authorization by reason and by hereditary prerogative.

. See note 1, same sec. of transcription.

passox 17, cont'd.

11. ēn hamāg ān kirbag hast kē abartarīh ud wuzurg mādagīh

rāy paymān handāzag.ud čand-š yazdān pad wisp āgāhīh

tuwān dānēstan.pad ān i mardōmān xrad dānišn anāyāb.

nswer 17, cont'd.

1. All these are the benefactions whose proportion, measure
and substantiability [only] deities[1] are able to know through
[their] omniscience: [it is] not ascertainable through men's
wisdom and intelligence.

. Whether the Pahlavi word 'yazdān' should be taken as plural of 'yazd'
or as singular by itself, has been the subject of some controversy. I
have kept the plural form throughout the translation of this book, because it seems to be the correct reflection of the Zoroastrian conception and usage of this word. Admitting the idea of monotheism with a
touch of dualism in Zoroastrianism, still the worshipping of other deities such as Mithra, Haoma, Sraoša and others is undeniable. Also, although Ahura Mazda alone is referred to as omniscient 'harvispāgāh',
yet other dieties are credited with many similar supernatural qualities
ascertaining their scope of knowledge beyond human capability. A few
examples are:

- In Yasna 10[a], Mithra is endowed with much perception, ibid. 61.
  He is immortal (ibid., 74). He is all-knowing (ibid., 82). No material
  man in existence is endowed with greater insight than that which supernatural Mithra has (ibid., 107).

- In Yašt 11[b], Sraoša is the incarnate word, ibid., 18. He is never
  sleeping, wakefully maintaining the creation of Mazdah (ibid., 11-12-
  13).

- In Yašt 12[c], Rašnu is most fore-seeing Rašnu, most knowing Rašnu,
  most fore-knowing Rašnu (ibid., 7).

- In Yašt 17[d], Aši brings heavenly wisdom at her wish, ibid. 2. She
  is with fullness of intellect (ibid., 23).

- In Yasna 9[e], Haoma keeps death away (ibid., 2). He gives complete
  knowledge (ibid., 17). He gives absolute comfort (ibid., 19).

(a) I. Gershevitch, Hymn to Mithra (Cambridge University Press,1959).
(b) SBE,XXIII, tr. Darmesteter.
(c) Ibid.

(d) Ibid.
(e) J. Unvala, Neryosangh's Sanskrit Version of Hōm Yašt, (Bombay,1924).
cont...

Answer 17, Note 1, cont'd.

So in order not to quit the realm of Zoroastrian divinities, while reading this text, let us keep to the originality of yazdān with the plural suffix-ān and do not concern ourselves with the ambiguity of post-Islamic references to this word either in Šāhnāmeh or Borhān-i Qāteᶜ or Farhang-i Moᶜin, in which yazdān is taken to mean "(the one) God".

passox 17, cont'd.

12. ud hangirdīg and dānistan šāyēd.kū tā ān hangām ka meh
     sūdīh ud frayādišn mardōm abārīg spenāg mēnōg dām az-š
     hamē bēd.kirbag az-š hamē rawēd.nōg nōg ēk abar did ha
     waxšēd ud abzāyēd.

13. ēn ān hast i.bē xwadān xwadā pāyagān[1] enyā kardan kam
     tuwān.

14. ēn kū. ka andar āwām-ē dō ayāb sē mad ēstēd.i kardan meh
     sūdīh.ud ēk šāyēd.xūbīh be nigerišn.ān i meh dādestānt
     kunišn.čē-š framān-iz-i weh dēn pad-š

---

1. [Pahlavi script] Ank. reads <u>khvatāe tāigān</u> , so does K.J., "Aspect:
    of Kirpak", <u>Memorial Jean De Menasce</u>, (Imprimerie Orientaliste,
    Louvain, 1974). I think the first letter of the second word must
    be corrupted form of ﻉ . To support my reading, H.K. Mirza pre-
    sented the following: Av. haẟānaēpata, Pahlavi tr., [Pahlavi script]
    (a transcript) with the variant [Pahlavi script] (Pahlavi. Y. 7-3, DH.
    p. 44).

Answer 17, cont'd.

12. In short, it suffices to know that much, that until
that time when great benefit and aid will come to mankind and other creatures of the Bounteous Spirit[1], good
deeds will issue therefrom again and again, one over
the other will ever grow and [will] increase.

13. The fact is that except for lords and those of lordly
ranks, others are less liable to be able to do it.

14. The explanation is this; at a time when two or three
benefactions coincide and it is possible to undertake
[only] one, then it should be carefully pondered, and
the one which is more lawful should be put into effect,
because this is a command of the Zoroastrian religion.

---

1. Pahlavi spenāg-mēnōg, the creative power of the world as opposed
to ganāg-mēnōg, the destructive power.

passox 17, cont'd.

15. kirbag kē-š ewāzīgīh frāy.ud ān-iz har dō pad-š
     pādixšā.weh dēn framānīh wēš kirbagīh.paydāgīgtar
     andar āstwānīh pad weh dēn.nōg nāvar yazišnīh.xwēdōdah
     warzišnīh.hamāg abestāg pad padisār yazišnīh.gāhānbār
     i hamāg[1] sāl pad gāh xwēš yazišnīh.ud sāzišnīh
     xwarišnīh ud dahišnīh.ud andar im rōzgārān zōhr ō
     ātaxš-i wahrām dahišnīh.ud ka yazišn-i dwāzdah-hōmāst
     wēš kirbagtar.ud amahrspandān šnāyišn az-š abērtar.ud
     abārīg frēzbān wizārišnīh i andar rōzgār ud māhīgānwār
     ud sālwār.kē hamāg kirbag ōwōn frayādišn-i ruwān az-š
     was mēnōgīhā.kū rōzan ud bōp[2] pad-š gētīgīha.ōwōn bē
     andar wehdēn.andāzag-ē ud paymān-ē paydāgīnēd ēstēnd.
     ayāb-š pad dānišnīh gētīgān and-iz šāyēd.

---

1.   K.J., "Aspects of Kirpak", Memorial Jean De Menasce, (Imprimerie
     Orientaliste, Louvain, 1974), reads xēm and translates nature.
     See plate, also NB. below.

2.   K.J.'s reading, op. cit., p. 242.

NB. After examining the MS, I believe it could be a mis-script of ᵇ⁾
     meaning the "same".

5. The more exclusive benefaction is also that which implies both religious commandments as well as the practice of more beneficial services according to religous law which would be more clearly manifested through religious trustworthiness. The ritual of nōg nāvar,[1] practicing of xwēdōdāh,[2] the ritual of the [recitation] of the whole Avesta from the beginning, the ritual of Gāhānbārs[3] all the year at their proper period, the ritual of the preparation of food and offerings, and offering libation to the Sacred Fire during day-time, and the ritual of dawāzdah-homāst[4] [which] is of great merit and paying homage to the Holy Immortals[5] which is [even] more than that: and other obligatory practices that regularly daily, monthly, and yearly are performed; are all benefactions which relieve the soul and are of very spiritual quality just as windows and carpets are of material [quality] in the [present] world. Thus, few measures and proportions have been explained in terms of religion; therefore in the light of understanding, people should observe as many [as possible].

. A ceremony for initiating a candidate in the priesthood. K.J.,"Aspects of Kirpak", Memorial Jean De Menasce, (Louvain, 1974), p.246, note 5.

. Marriage among relations.

. The six divisions of the year; the five-day festivals celebrated at the ends of these.

. A ceremony performed in honor or in memory of women either living or dead. Modi, The Religious Ceremonies of Parsees, (Bombay,1922), pp.431-33.

. The six spiritual beings created by Ohrmazd, namely: Wahman, Ardwahist, Šahrewar, Spandarmad, Hordād, Amurdād.

passox 17, cont'd.

16. andar-iz ēn.hast har kas kardan nē tuwān.

17. hamē andar mardōm.ōy pad huxrad dārišn.kē.pad hangām
    i xwēštan.bunīg nigerišnīha.andar āmār dārēd.menišnīgīh
    kirbag-i frēzbānīg.wināh dušmenīhā ud ruwān az-š
    bōzenītārīh.pad awizīrišnīgīh.kirbag i ul frēzbānīg.
    mēnōgān dōšaramīhā.kirbag handōxtārīh.ud ruwān abartar
    gāh winārdārīh ud kirbag frāxwinārdārīh wināh
    wigārišn kāmagīhā rāy.tuwān sāmānīhā kunēd.

18. ēd hast.andar gētīg ud mēnōg.frayādištom.yazdān kām
    kunišn.ēn-iz hast.ō ruwān ayārīh ud tan husrawīh.wuzurg
    sūd.

19. kē.ruwān dōšāram rāy.az wināh pahrēzēd.nē kunēd.pad
    dušhumat dušhūxt dušhuwaršt.andar mēnōgān ud gētīgān
    any yazdān xwēš ruwān gētīgīg zāhagān zāgān hamtōhmagān
    ud hamahlān[1] ēraxtag ud druxtag hamēmālōmand nē.

---

1. Ank. reads hamiyāran . K.J. reads hambrātān ,"Aspects of Kirpak",
   Memorial Jean De Menasce, (Louvain, 1974). See plate.

16. However, there are [certain benefactions] which are not
practicable for everybody.

17. Always, of all men, that one would be considered wise who
in his own time, with profound contemplation regards the
obligatory benefactions favorably (menišnīgha) and [con-
siders] sin with hostility (duš-menišnīgha), owing to
which his soul will be redeemed. [He is considered the
wise one] who does inevitably within his possibilities
the obligatory benefaction with love for the Spirits, [in
order] to acquire benefactions, and to obtain a superior
place for the soul and to amass meritorious deeds with
the desire for the remission of [his] sins.

18. To act accordingly to the will of deities, is the great-
est support in the material and spiritual world. It also
is of great benefit to aid the soul, [and to create] physical
soundness for the body.

19. He who for esteem of the soul does not commit sin through
abstaining from evil thoughts, evil words, and evil deeds toward spiritual and material beings and other deities, and
toward his [own] soul and toward the four elements of
nature[1] and her offspring, and to relatives and associates,
will not be afflicted [or] deceived, and will not have
enemies.

. Water, fire, earth, air.

pass͟o͟x͟ ͟1͟7͟, cont'd.

20.   ud pad hamāg menišnīgīhā.abaxšīhā paydāg.gōwišn andčand
       šāyēd.pad-iz kunišn.wināh wizārdār būdan.

21.   ēn gyāg.nigerēd kū.har ān kirbag.i pad gētīg xīr
       xwēsēnīdan šāyēd.andčand xwēsēnēd az gētīg xīr.weh ud
       mādagōmandtar ud pādāyišnīgtar.čē gētīg xīr.ka-iz
       was   andar iz diz-i ōstwār dārihēd.hamāg sazišnīg
       hanjafišnīg ud wišufišnīg.ō xwēsan ud axwēsān rasišnig.
       kāmagōmandīhā ud akāmagīhā.uš ō mēnōg ud ganj-i yazdān
       šawēd.anōh.frayādag.ō wehān arzānīgān.rādīhā ud ahlāyīh
       dōšāramīhā.dahīhēd.ayāb.abar ān-i spenagmēnōg gētīg-dām
       uš meh sūdīh uzihēd.čē ān i jāwēdānīgīhā asazišn.

22.   ōwōn saxwan warzīdār nē judāgīhēd.ud kas-iz az-š judāg
       kardan nē tuwān. uš hamē pad xwēšīh estišnīg pad
       winārišnīg.

Answer 17, cont'd.

20. And with all one's heart, repentance should be manifested
    in [one's] words and deeds [in order] to be redeemed from
    sin.

21. At this juncture, bear in mind that whatever benefaction
    which you can appropriate to yourself in worldly goods,
    appropriate with worldly goods, which are the best, the
    most legal and the most enduring. Because even if you
    keep the material wealth in a strong fortress it is all
    perishable, finite and destructible, whether it falls
    in the hands of relatives or non-relatives, willingly or
    unwillingly, ultimately it will go to the spirit and
    the treasure of the deities. There, it will be given,
    as a matter of help to good deserving people with gene-
    rosity and love of righteousness. Therefrom a great
    benefit will reach the worldly creation of the Bounteous
    Spirit [creative power of the world], as it is everlasting-
    ly imperishable.

22. He who practices [according to] such statements is not
    separated [from his material wealth], and no one can
    separate him therefrom. It is always in his possession
    by law of nature.

passox 17, cont'd.

23.   ud ēn xīr gētīg.az ahlāyīh ud ruwān dōšāram rāy.dahīhēd.

ōwōn abāyēd dādan kū-š abēzagīhā.xwēš gētīgīhā.mēnōgīhā

kas-iz pad-š nē hamemālōmand. ud az awizīrišnīg frēzbān

wizārišnīh i-š dēnīgīhā.i ō-iz ōy frayād ēstēd.čē.ēn-iz.

abāg awizīrišnīg ud frēzbānīg wizārišnīh.abardom kirbag.

24.   mardom ēn-iz āmārēnīdan sazēd kū mard.hast pad hangām kū

pādixšā.kū bahr-i tan-i xwēš.ruwān dōšāram rāy.bē ō any

abārīg.dahēd.nē padixšā kū.ān frēzbān dahišn i ōy kē-š

frēzbānīg.ō-iz ōy awizīrišnīgīhā abāyišnīg:be ō anē ēd

arzānīgtar dahēd.az ān čē.frēzbānīg ō-iz ōy.uš frēzbānīg

dēn framānīhā.čē.ka dahēd.wināh wēš kū kirbag.ka ān.dahē

rāy.dēnīg frezbānīg wizārišnīh rāy.šāyēd kardan.

Answer 17, cont'd.

23. And this material wealth is dedicated with righteousness
for esteem of the soul. So, it should be given with
holiness, from one's own material and spiritual [posses-
sion], with no one having any objection to it. And it
is from the inevitable, obligatory deeds prescribed by
the religion that he [the practitioner of the above-mentioned benefactions] will get secours, because fulfil-
ment of obligatory duty is the supreme benefaction.

24. People should also bear in mind that there are times
when, for the sake of esteem for the soul, people are
entitled to give a share of their own wealth to some other
deserving person. [But] it would not be lawful if that
obligatory charity of him upon whom it is incumbent to
give, be given to another who is needier. Because it
is incumbent upon him, and this is by command of the religion. If he gives [otherwise], the sin is greater than
the good deed. It should be given as a gift and as a
religious obligation.

passox 17, cont'd.

25. ud ēn i-mān azabar uzwārd.hangird paydāgenīdārīh ēd i

abar frēzbānīg ud afrēzbānīg-iz kirbag warzidārīh.kē

dānāgān was hangōšidag handāzag.i pad ahlāyīh warzīdārī

abāyišnīg.uš āwurdan dānistan šāyēd pad yazdān ayārīh.

26. ud ān-i abar wirāstan-i puhl-ē abar hušk rōd-ē.pad

nāmčist.nibišt.šnāxtan ēn.čiyōn-tān kirbag-ē.i wuzurg

mādag ud purr frayād-i amaragān sūd.mad ēstēd.kunēd.

27. tā ka hast mardōmān.az-š frayādišn.ud kirbag az-š

rawišnīg.ud a-š dahišn abēr mādagōmandtar frayādišnīgt

kū dō hazār wināh pādīrān.i ān pādīrānīh rāy.frēzbān

wizārišnīh.ēd rāy.pargūd ēstēd.enyā.ka-š.ān pādīrānīh

nē any frēzbān wizārišnīh pargūd ēstēd.saxwan pad-š

juttar.

5.   What we have pointed out above, was a brief illustra-
       tion of obligatory, as well as of voluntary practice
       of benefaction. It is expected that the sensible ones
       should practice in many similar ways and in proportions
       by way of righteousness. Notification and recognition
       of it [i.e. obligatory and voluntary benefactions] is
       necessary. By the help of the deities.

6.   As for the construction of a bridge over a dry river
       bed   [about which it] is written in particular,[1] you
       are to consider it [an opportunity for] a benefaction
       of great importance, very helpful and of public benefit,
       which has arisen.

7.   As long as mankind will exist, men will benefit from
       it, and benefaction will continue. This charity [i.e.
       the actual construction of a bridge] is more substan-
       tial and more useful than 2000 abstentions from sins
       which might exempt a man from his obligatory deed. The
       advice would be different, when obligatory deeds are
       not exempted by abstention from sin.

---

1.   Among the enumeration of penalties to be paid by one who kills
       another (Vd. 14.16) or has intercourse with a menstruous woman
       (Vd. 18.74) is the building of bridges over canals. K.J.,
       "Aspects of Kirpak", Memorial Jean De Menasce, (Louvain, 1974),
       p. 248, note 11.

28. čē puhl-i pad ēn ēwēnag.ka-iz amaragān sūd.abar xwadāyān
frēzbānīg.ud ušān kardan niyābagtar awišān kunišnīgtar
ud pad sazāgtar.

29. pas az xwadāyān ō abārīg amaragānīgān kunišnīgtar.ka-šān
abāyēd kardan.pad hamēh kardan čimīg kārīhātar.

30. amaragān mardōm ān amaragānīg kār ēwtāgīhā ōwōn kunišn.
kū-š im kunišn rāy.ān i-š dēnīg.pad kardan abar frēzbān
uš pargūd nē bēd.az-iz zyān az uzwāhīgīh ud awērānišn i
pad-š šāyēd būdan. xwēštan abēzārenitan tuwān.

31. ō-iz weh dēn mardom.andar puhl anāg āwām.hamāg kirbag i
mardōm kunēnd.meh ud keh.ud amaragānīg ēwāzīg.frēzbānig
ud afrēzbānig.ān pāhlom ud nēktom ud frayādišnīgtom.i
ruwān hambrādagīhā ud ahlāyīhā frēhīhā.pad sūd ud
abartargāhīh ud purr urwahmīh-i ruwān.kunīhēd.ayāb kirb
dōšāram rāy.i hast ān pāhlom ud ān abēzagtar.i ō
fradāyīšn-i ruwān rasišnīgtar pad srōšdārīh.pad dastwar
abēzag dēn dastwarān kunēnd.

nswer 17, cont'd.

8. Since a bridge of such nature would entail public benefit, it is the obligatory duty of the lords and would
be more appropriate and more fitting to be achieved by
them.

9. Next to the lords, stand other common people in aptness
[for the job]. Team work achievement is more purposeful.

0. The comunity of men must perform public work individually
in such a way that for this work, that which is religious
and is obligatory to be performed will not be dispersed
for him, and as a result of that [participation] he can
redeem himself from damages and extra ravages which could
possibly befall him.

1. Also, for adherents of Zoroastrian religion in this evil
time of punishment, of all benefactions that people do:
great, small, public, exclusive, obligatory, voluntary,
that one is the most sublime, the best, the most helpful
which is performed in association of soul and with extreme
righteousness in the light of [bestowing] benefit, exalta-
tion and blissfulness of the soul. Or for the love of
benefaction, which is sublime and holy and is more reliev-
ing to the soul, [behave] obediently and canonically [ac-
cording] to what the authorities of the holy religion do.

123

32. rad dastwar pad rad dastwar menēd ud dārēd.ud rad dastw

     menīšnīgīhā dāštan pad dād dārēd.uš menīšnīgīhā dāštan

     pad dād dārēd.uš menīšnīgīhā ed-iz pad dād dāšt ēstēd

     kū.ka rad dastwar pad rad dastwar nē dārēd.šāyēd.ēg-š

     kirbag i kunēd.pad rāh-i asrōīhdārīh[1].pad mēnōgān ō

     frayād nē rasēd.ka-š was-iz kard ēstēd.ēg-š az-š ēdōn

     dūr bēd.čiyōn ka andar gētīg čiš-iz kirbag nē kard ēstē

33. pad abestāg gugāhīh.nē kas ān i āsrōīhdār mard. kē dast

     nē dārēd.uš dād-iz ē kū nē abāyēd dāštan.ēg nē rasēd ō

     ān i pāhlom axwān.nē ka ōy ān and abar ōšmārišnīh hē.

     kū-šān kār ud kirbag ān and kard ēstēd.čand spīg-i

     urwarān.kē pad wahār frāz waxšēd ēstēd.kē-š dād was spī

     Ohrmazd.

---

1.   Ank. and K.J. read asrōšdār, "Aspects of Kirpak", Memorial Jean De
      Menasce, (Louvain, 1974), p. 243.

Answer 17, cont'd.

32. Regard and respect religious masters and religious
    authorities as masters and authorities and consider it
    as a duty. Because if one does not respect masters and
    authorities duly and thinks that it would be lawful not
    to regard masters and authorities appropriately, then
    any benefaction he performs with the intention of re-
    spect to priesthood, would not be of any help. Even if
    he performs many [of these benefactions] they will stay
    so far from him as though he had never achieved any bene-
    faction in this world.

33. According to Avestic evidence, he who does not respect
    religious authorities is not considered a man of [re-
    spect for] charity. He whose creed is that religious au
    thorities should not be revered will never attain a
    noble life, even if the account of the meritorious deeds
    he has fulfilled equals the sprouts of the plants that
    grow forth in the spring, the plants 'which' Ohrmazd gave
    so many sprouts.

passox 17, cont'd.

34. ēn-iz guft hē.nē kas ān i āsrōīhdan[1] kē dastwar nē dārēd

aš ahlāyīh ān i ō ruwān tōzišn wānēd.[2] kū kirbag wināh

nē kanēd uš nē-iz mustkārih ō hamdārēd.kū-š az dušox nē

bōzēd.

---

1. Ank. amends to ‏پروردار‎ āsrušt.

2. Ank. reads kunēt.

Answer 17, cont'd.

34. This is also [a canonical] statement that no man is
     [considered] a man of charity who does not revere the
     religious authorities, his rightousness will not balance
     out his atonement for the soul. That is to say [his]
     benefaction will not counteract his faults. Neither
     would rebelliousness [from this fact] be of any avail.
     That is, he will not be redeemed from hell.

pursišn 18

1. mard-ē.kē stūr padīruft xwāstag pad im stūrīh stānēd.
    čiyōn andar dēn paydāg.

2. im mard pādixšā ka im xwāstag uzēnag kunēd.ayāb uš az
    nīrmad uzēnag kardan abāyēd.agar-š nīrmad nē bawēd.
    čiyōn abāyēd kardan.

3. agar frazand.kē stūr bawēd.nē zāyēd.mard dah sāl kam
    wēš.pad har kār tuxšišn kunēd.uš frazand nē zāyēd.ān
    drahm kē stad abāz pas abāyēd dādan ayāb nē.

Question 18

1. What is the religious declaration regarding the
   money[1] that a man receives [as a trust] when he accepts
   stūrīh?[2]

2. Is this man entitled to spend this money or should he
   spend the interest of that money? If there is no interest [on that money], what should be the procedure?

3. If the offspring who is the stūr has no issue but tries
   his best for about ten years, more or less, [to produce
   a child] yet he is childless; should he give back the
   money [drahm] he has received or not?

---

1.   xwāstag generally means "object" in the legal sense of the word, in most cases, however, "money" is understood by the word. See C. Bartholomae, NSL., (1931), XVIII, 45, note 1.

2.   References are already given in Question 1, note 5. as to the details of stūrīh and stūr. Also notes 1. and 2. and N.B. of Answer 1 deal with the same question. For the sake of convenience the following would be a brief summarization: the word stūr in Pahlavi texts covers different aspects of guardianship and proxyhood. Various interpretations are given by western scholars already mentioned above. Parsi scholars have given definitions of the same, pertinent to whatever case it might occur. There are various cases to which stūr and stūrīh apply. In this particular text, whenever stūr is not translated into English it conveys that particular aspect of the word which means an adopted son or daughter who in addition to the responsibility of productivity in terms of maintaining the lineage, acts as a proxy for the procuration of family capital as well.

pursišn 18, cont'd.

4.   ud agar mard zan widarān šawēnd dādestān-i ān stūr
     čē.

5.   ud ēn mard kē stūrīh rāyēnīdan padīruft aš čiš-iz miz[
     nīrmad bawēd ayāb nē.agar bawēd.ān sturīh drahm[1] az
     kē stāndan.

6.   ka abāz bē dah sāl-iz tā az kū gyāg.agar farzand zāyē[
     ō dād pānzdah sālag nē rasēd.dādestān-i im drahm ud
     mard čē.ud agar rasēd.pas widarān šawēd.pid ud mād az
     stūrīh abēzār bawēnd.ayāb-šān dādestān čē.

---

1.   To render proper meaning an _ʰ_ should be interpolated. Men.,
     Feux et Fondations pieuses dans le droit Sassanide, (Paris, 1964)
     p. 40, has translated without az which makes the point sensele

.   If the man and the woman [husband and wife who have appointed this stūr] both pass away, what would be the legal
situation of this stūr?

.   [Under the circumstances] would there be any salary or any
gain for this man who has accepted to exercise as a stūr
[for them] or not? And if there is any [salary], from
whom should it be obtained?

.   However, if later [within] some ten years hence, a child
is born [i.e. to the stūr] who does not survive until the
age of fifteen; what would be the legal situation of that
money as well as that of the man, and if he (the child)
reaches [the age of fifteen] and then passes away, would
the parents be discharged from stūrīh? What would be the
legal status?

passox 18

7. agar-š čiš andar nēst ān rāy juttar.hangirdīg ēn kū.
    xwāstag-i stūrīh.kē hamāg be nigāh ud pad gyāg dāštan.
    ōwōn ku-š čiš-e-iz kamīh pad-š andar nē āyēd.sē stīr
    drahm hast.ān weh ka barōmand bawēd.

8. az sē stīr i pad bun xwāstag-i stūrīh uzēnīdan ud
    kāstan nē pādixšā ud tuwān sāmānīhā barōmand dārišn.

9. ān i az sē stīr wēš.pad čār ud tuwān ōwōn kunišn kū
    barōmand bawēd.az bar uzēnag kunēd.

Answer 18

7.   If there is nothing else implied in this question which
     would require another answer, the following would be a
     brief explanation. The [minimum amount of] money in trust
     which should be always kept attentively, subject to no
     reduction, is three stīr drahm[1] and it would be preferable
     if it be interest-bearing.

8.   From that total sum of the money in trust, no reduction
     or expenditure is allowed and one ought to be able to
     keep it prolific within its limits.

9.   That [money in trust] which exceeds three stīrs, one
     should exert all one's power and ability in such a way
     to make it more profitable. Expenditure should be made
     out of the interest [of that money in trust].

---

1.   See answer 3, note **3**.

133

passox 18, cont'd.

10.   agar-š bar pad uzēnag awizīrišnīg nē bunīg.tā abāz ō
       sē stīr āyēd.pad ān i awizīrišnîg.az xīr.pādixšā uzēnē
       i az-š[1] pad uzēnag-i rōzgārīg im stūrīh rāyēnīdan.
       sīnag-masāy ud bāzā-masāy wastargīg wahāg.čiyōn ān i
       dūdagsālār rāy nibišt.xwēšihēd.

11.   ān-iz xwāstag-i pad stūrīh stad ēstēd.ka-iz abēr was
       pad bun.pahrēzōmandīhā barōmand dārišn.

12.   uš and čand sīnag-masāy ud bāzā -masāy wastargīg wahāg
       i-š xwēš uzēnag kunišn.

13.   uš xwāstag-i sturīh.zīndagīh dranāy.ō dārišn.

_____

1.   Ank. reads uš.

Answer 18, cont'd.

10.   If the interest is absolutely not sufficient for the
expenses, on the grounds of this necessity, it would be
lawful to spend from the capital money to the limit of the
three stīr level, from which a portion should be taken
daily for daily expenses of this curation.[1] [i.e. the
salary of the proxy, for his handling the money in
trust]. That is taking from it as much as both ends
would meet, as already explained [in the chapter] on
family guardianship.[2]

11.   As for the money which is held in trust, even if it is
[a] substantial [amount], it should be preserved profi-
tably with care.

12.   And he (i.e. the proxy) should spend [from it] for his
personal needs only to the extent that both ends meet.

13.   And he (i.e. the proxy) should preserve that money which
is in his trust, all through his life.

---

1.   stūrīh, see C. Bartholomae, NSL., (1936), XXX, 70.

2.   See answer 5, sec. 15, note 1.

135

passox 18, cont'd.

14.   agar zan pad im stūrīh gīrēd.ud az-š frazand zāyēd.ag
        pus.stūrīg pus i ōy kē-š stūrīh az-š padīruft ēstēd.

15.   ka pus ō dād-i pānzdah sālag mad.ēg-š rāyēnīdan-i im
        stūrīh bowandagīnīdan ud xwāstag-i stūrīh be ō im pus
        rasēd.pad xwēšīh be awīš abespārišn.

16.   agar im pus.pas az dād-i pānzdah sālagīh frāz rawēd.u
        xwāstag hast.stūr abāyēd gumārdan.ud stūrīh ān i[1] tā
        gumārišn.ud[2] ān pus gumārd.stūrīh-iz ān pēš andar-š.

---

1.   Ank.amends to ōy .

2.   Ank. amends to tā .

Answer 18, cont'd.

14. If he [i.e. the man who has been chosen a _stūr_] takes
a wife during[1] this _stūrīh_ and [she] gives birth to a
child; if it is a boy the _stūrīh_ of the boy goes to the
person from whom he [the father of this son] has accepted
the _stūrīh_. [i.e. their first son belongs to the person
who had adopted the father of this newborn son as an
adopted son. Here lies the philosophy of maintaining
the lineage].

15. If this boy reaches the age of fifteen, then he ought
to undertake the administration of this curation and the
money in trust will go to him. It should be handed over
to him as his own property.

16. In case this boy passes away after the age of fifteen
and he possesses [some] property; a proxy should be
assigned [for him]. This curation continues until a[n
adopted] son is assigned [for the deceased]. When this
[adopted] son is assigned, he also becomes amenable to
the previous stūrīh [i.e. the stūrīh status of the de-
ceased].

---

1.   Men., _Feux et Fondations pieuses dans le droit Sassanide_, (Paris, 1964),
p. 41, translates "si l'on prend une femme qui a une stūrīh" which
seems unjustified.

137

passox 18, cont'd.

17.   ud agar-š pus nē bē duxt.zāyēd.stūrīh nē pad raft dār
        pad im ēwēnag.pad im mard ud zan be ēstēd.

18.   agar har dō farāz rawēnd.uš ān frazand ēwāz ān duxt h
        i ayōkēn-i ōy.kē-š stūrīh az-š padīruft ēstēd.bawēd.
        xwāstag-i im stūrīh hamāg be awiš rasēd.

19.   agar pus ud duxt-ē čand bawēnd ka ēk az pusarān ō pān
        sālagīh mad.dūdagsālārīh ōy-šān pus duxt bawēd.ušān
        xwāstag-i stūrīh pusīhā ud duxtīhā xwēšihēd.

20.   ud ka pus hast.duxt ayōkēn nē bawēd.

21.   ud ka pus nēst.duxt wēš kū ēk.ušān ēk ayōkēn.ān i pad
        ayōkēnīh be ēstēd.az im xwāstag.pusīhā.ud abārīg duxt
        stānišn.

138

Answer 18, cont'd.Answer 18, cont'd.

17. If it is not a boy [the child who is born to this
     already stūr], but is a girl who has been born, stūrīh
     should not be considered gone to her [i.e. she is not
     entitled to that as the boy was] [but] will remain the
     responsibility of the husband and wife [i.e. her par-
     ents].

18. If both of them [i.e. husband and wife] pass away and
     their only child is that girl, [she will become] ayōkēn
     to the person who had been the proxy [of her parents].
     The property and the money in trust go entirely to him
     [i.e. the same proxy who has taken her as ayōkēn].

19. If there are several boys and girls; when one of the
     boys reaches the age of fifteen, he will become the
     family guardian of other boys and girls and will bring
     the property and the money in trust to his own possession.

20. And if there is a boy, the girl will not become an ayōkēn.

21. And if there is no boy and the [number of] girls is more
     than one, one of them becomes ayōkēn. The one who has
     become ayōkēn should take according to boy's portion from
     the property and the other girl should take according to
     girl's portion.

139

22.   bē ān i pad ayōkēnīh be ēstēd.ēnyā abārīg pádixšaīhā
       zan bawēd.

23.   kē-š zan gīrēd.agar-šān zindagīh dranāy frazand nē
       bawēd.tā ēk az-šān zindag.stūrīh pad ōy i zindag
       hastišnīg.

24.   ka har dō widarān bawēnd.ušān frazand nēst.xwāstag-i
       stūrīh be ō ōy rasēd.kē andar dūdag-i ōy kē stūrīh ōy
       rāy bawēd.i-š nazdīk paywandtar ud sazāgtar pad stūrī
       ōy.uš pad stūrīh ōy dārišn.

Answer 18, cont'd.

22.   Except the one who is ay$\bar{a}$kēn, the other girl is [en-
         titled to] pādīxš$\bar{a}$ wifeship.

23.   If [someone] takes her [i.e. the pādixš$\bar{a}$ one] as a
         wife, but produces no child during their lifetime, as
         long as one of them is alive, curation is due upon the
         one who is alive.

24.   If both of them pass away and there is no issue left
         from them, curation of the money goes to a person in
         his family [i.e. the family of the dead person] who is
         eligible to be proxy. He who is the next of kin and
         is the most worthy for curation, he should be regarded a
         st$\bar{u}$r.

pursišn 19

1. garmābag-i akdēnān.kē-š šōyišn i āb az-š be āb i rawāg
    būd.agar mard-i weh dēn andar awiš šawēd.a-š čiš pad-š
    be wardēd ayāb nē.

2. agar be zamīg wišād šawēd.kē-š xwaršēd abar tābēd.čiyōn
    bawēd.

3. agar nē šāyēd.ka mard wēmār bawēd ud bizešk hamē gōwēd
    kū be garmābag šaw.šāyēd ka šawēd ayāb nē.

Question 19

1. The Moslem[1] bath-house, which is for washing [one-self] and where its water is [supplied by] flowing water; if a Zoroastrian[2] goes there, would it make any difference or not?

2. If he goes [afterwards] to the open air where sun shines upon the earth, how would it be [interpreted religiously]?

3. If not lawful, what would be the situation when a person is sick and the physician recommends that the patient should go to the bath-house? Should he go or not?

---

1. See Question 1, note 3.
2. See Question 1, note 2.

pursišn 19, cont'd.

4.   agar nē šāyēd ud rawēd.āb awiš be barēnd[1] ud azēr-i pāy
   be abganēnd tā-š gyān abar lab jahēd[2].āb pad tan frāz nē
   hilēd.šāyēd ayāb nē.

---

1.   See   tr. note 2, line 9, for the expression of "āb awiš burdan".

2.   BTE. ǀ𐫰𐫇ǀ Ank. reads šēt. It seems to be corrupted form of ǀ𐫰𐫇ǀ
   See plate.

Question 19, cont'd.

4.   If it is not permissible and he goes [not with the inten-
       tion of washing himself but only for benefitting from
       the heat of the bath house] and someone brings the water
       to him [from the reservoir of the bath house] and throws
       the water under his feet, [pouring water upon him by
       force], to the extent that his life comes up to his lips[1],
       yet he does not submit to water being poured upon him.
       Is this [stubbornness] acceptable or not[2]?

---

1.   Jān abar lab jastan is a common expression in present colloquial
     Persian denoting "having a very hard time". (tr's. note)

2.   To be able to follow the point in this sec., one must be familiar
     with the old Persian system of public bath houses which were in use
     even until a few decades ago. There was a relatively large
     sauna room, the temperature of which was quite warm without having
     steam. Inside this big sauna room there were two big built-in wa-
     ter reservoirs one for cold water and one for hot water. The char-
     coal or wood boiler, which was built under the hot water reservoir and
     had to be fed from outside, generated heat to all parts of this so-
     called sauna. There were special attendants whose job was to fetch
     water from these reservoirs and fill the buckets of each individual
     who wanted to wash himself. These buckets were usually supplied by the
     bath-house manager. But sometimes people used to take their own. When
     the procedure of washing was completed, there was an adjacent room
     where people dried themselves and put on their clothes. Very often
     people used to go and spend a short while in the sauna section only
     for the sake of warmth and relaxation especially people with muscle
     and bone pains.

passox 19

5. garmābag-i akdēnān.har čiyōn kunēd.āb ō har kū šawēd.
pad hixrōmand ēwar ud pad nasā pāsīh warōmand.čē ōyšān
pahrēz-i hixr ud nasā az āb ud ātaxš pad kēš nēst.

6. weh dēn ō garmābag-i akdēnān šudan.kirb pad-š šustan.
ne dastwarīhā.

7. kē kunēd.ud agar-iz wēmārīh rāy hē.eg-š tan pad rēman
dārišn ud pad pēšag šǫyišn.

8. wehdēnān ka-šān garmābag čiš-ē hast awizīrīšnīgīhā pad
kār abāyēd.xwad rāy ē wirāyēnd.čē.garmābag čiš-ē hast kē
nē ēn akdēnān ō dīdan āwurd.ušān az kardag-i pēšēnīgān
frāz gīrift.

9. and⬛⬛huxwadāyīh hangām.pad nazdīkīh-i ātaxšgāhīhā ud
gāh⬛⬛bār kadagīhā.garmābag wirāst ēstēd.

Answer 19

A Moslem bath house, whatever way it functions and where
ever its water comes from it is polluted for sure and is
susceptible to [lack of] dead matter precautions. Because
there is no such rule in their religion regarding the protection of water and fire from excrement and dead matter.

Going·to the bath house of the Moslems and washing the
body there is not lawful for the Zoroastrians.

Whoever does it, even if on the account of illness, his
body should be considered polluted and should be washed
professionally [i.e., with a knotted stick - for details
of this purification rite see glossary, pad pēšaq šustan].

If there is an absolute need for the Zoroastrians to have
a bath, they should arrange for one themselves. Because
the bath house is not something [an idea] that Moslems
have introduced. They themselves have adopted it from
their forerunners.

At the time of the good rule,[1] establishing the bath house
near the fire temples and gāhānbār places was a common
practice.

The expression andar huxwadāyīh, "at the time of good lordship,"
refers to the Sassanian period, a common expression often encountered in Pahlavi texts.

147

passox 19, cont'd.

10. andar weh dēn paydāg kū ōy kē yazišn-i yazdān kāmēd

kardan.fradom xwēštan andar garmābag ē šōyēd.xwēštan

andar garmābag āb yōjdahr ē kūnēd.ud čiyōn pākīzagīhātar

hubōytar ō yazišn-i yazdān franāwēd.

Answer 19, cont'd.

10.   It is a religious declaration that he who wants to
[perform the rite to] worship deities, must go to the
bath-house first to wash himself. He should wash himself in the bath with clean water so that he could proceed with his worshipping of the deities in a cleaner,
better smelling state.

pursišn 20

1. mard-ē kē xwarišn-i garm andar dahān nihēd.uš dahān be sōzēd.xwarēd.

2. paymānag-i sōzišn kē-š rēmanīh az-š bawēd čiyōn.

3. paymānag-i nasā sōzēd pad handām čiyōn.

passox 20

4. andāzag-i dahān andarōn.kē-š rēmanīh pad-š bawēd.ān i ka.ān gyāg kū sōzēd.xōn pad-š abar āyēd.xwarišn kē-š sōzišn pad-š bawēd.ka hamē ōbārēd.ēn ōbārišn rāy.ēg-š tan rēman.

5. uzwān abārīg gyāg andar dahān pad ēn dar rāy hamāg ēwton

6. ka xōn nē paydāyīhēd.ābilag gīrēd.ka-iz pas huškābēd hixr xwarišnīh bawēd.rēman nē[1] kunēd.

7. pad abārīg handām.sōzišn-i pad ātaxš kē tan rēman kunēd ka abāg sōzišn xōn abar āyēd rēman ōh kunēd.

---

1. I think this <u>nē</u> is mis-script. I have omitted it in my translation.

Question 20

1. A man puts a hot [mouthful of a] meal in his mouth and his mouth is burned. [Yet] he eats it.

2. What is the proportion of burning which would result in pollution [of the mouth]?

3. What is the proportion of a scald on the external parts of the body which would cause pollution?

Answer 20

4. [The proportion equals] the size of the cavity of mouth where pollution has occured. That is, when that spot is burned it would bleed. When this burning [which has caused bleeding] is swallowed, the same swallowing would pollute the body.

5. This applies to the [injury of] the tongue or any other part of the mouth.

6. If it does not bleed, a blister will develop. When [the blister] dries up, the dead mucous membrane will be eaten (swallowed). It will cause pollution.

7. As for other external parts of the body, when burnt by fire, they will pollute the body. [That is to say], burning will develop bleeding, and thus it will result in pollution.

pursišn 21

1. rad kē wizīr-ē kunēd.ān i nē rēman rēman kunēd.ān gowēd
    kū.ka az any dastwar pursēd.juttar gōwēd.pad dastwar
    dārišn ayāb nē.ud tōzišn čē abāyēd kardan.wizīrīnīdan
    framāyēd pad yazdān kām.

passox 21

2. agar-š čiš andar nēst ān rāy juttar; ān kē kas i pad ha
    sē čāštag nē rēman.pad rēmanīh wizīr pad-š kunēd.pad
    dastwar nē šāyēd.

3. ud agar.pad ēk az sē čāštag rēman.ud pad ān čāštag wizī
    kunēd juttarīh ē pad-š nēst.

4. ān rad.kē kas i nē rēman pad rēmanīh wizīr pad-š kunēd.
    ēg-š zamānīg wīnāh bawēd tanāpuhl-ē.

Question 21

1. [Assume] a high priest who gives a judgement delivers
    his opinion on something which is not polluted, as pol-
    luted, and says that he had consulted with another judge.
    [And] he declares contradictions. Should he be regarded a
    judge or not? What he ought to do regarding atonement
    [of his false decision]. Please deliver us your comments
    by the grace of God.[1]

Answer 21

2. If there is nothing else implied in the question which
    would require another answer, the point is this: he who
    gives a perverse decision, on three occasions, for some-
    thing which is not polluted, as polluted, does not
    deserve judgeship.

3. If one out of three [occasions] holds and he gives [right]
    judgement on that one [still] it makes no difference [re-
    garding his unworthiness].

4. That high priest who offers wrong judgement on someone
    who is not polluted, has committed a tanāpuhl sin at that
    very moment.

---

1. See note 1, p. 248.

5. har wizend ud rēš zyān.az im wizīr.pad im kas bawēd.ō
bun-i im wizīr.uš ō ān mard tōzišn.

6. ān i ka gōwēd.kū-m az im dastwar pursēd.juttar gōwēd.
nigerišn pad-š.čē agar.jud čāštag rāy.pad-š juttar.abāg
čāštag-ē i az sē čāštag rāst andāzagīhā.ud agar.nē jud
čāštagīha bē drō wizīrīh rā ō bun.pad andāzag-i wizīr
i-š kard.

154

.   Any damage, harm or loss which would affect this person
    owing to this wrong judgement, would afflict the soul
    of the judge and he should atone to that man.

.   What he [the unworthy judge] says should be carefully
    examined, because if it is [the question of] different
    interpretation [of doctrines and teachings] the case
    would be different from [the case of] one right judge-
    ment out of three. And if it is not the question of
    false decision, that would be different [too]. In the
    latter case the sin of false judgement would afflict the
    soul and its proportion depends on the [importance of
    the] judgement he has made.

155

pursišn 22

1. mard-ē kē-š xwahar-ē hast.uš andar hangām ēd guft būd.
   kū.xwahar pad zanīh gīrēm.[1]ayāb-š az mādar ud pidar
   padīraft būd.kū.xwahar pad zanīh gīrēd.[2]pas nē gīrēd.
   wihānag-ē rāy rōzgār pad-š be widarēd.pas.mard-ē ān
   mard frāz gīrēd ud gōwēd.kū.xwahar ēn pad kirbag-i man.
   pad zanīh gīr tā tān drahm awiš dahēm.gīrēd.drahm frāz
   gīrēd.

2. ēn mard kē brād drahm dād.uš kirbag-i xwēdōdah bawēd
   ayāb nē.čiyōn.agar ēn guft.i pēš būd nē dānēd.mard nē
   gowēd.kū-m.az padīrišn ēd kardag hast.ēg-š dādestān be
   wardēd ayāb nē.

---

1. Ank. reads <u>kunom</u> .
2. Ank. reads <u>kunom</u> .

Question 22

1. There was a man who had a sister. Once he said,
   "I will marry this sister." [and] his parents had
   agreed that he would marry his sister. Later on he did
   not execute the deed, and for some reasons, days passed
   like that. Then someone told him [the brother],"On
   behalf of my meritorious deed, marry your sister, and
   I will pay you for that." He [the brother] did so and
   received the money.

2. Is there any share of benefaction of xwēdōdāh[1] for this
   man who offered money to the brother to perform the
   meritorious deed of xwēdōdāh, or not. What if he [the
   man who offered money] was not aware of what that brother had said before [regarding his marriage with his
   sister] and he [the brother] had not told him [the man
   offering money] that he had accepted [promised] this
   engagement. Would it change the situation from the
   religious viewpoint or not?

---

1. Next of kin marriage.

<u>passox 22</u>

3.   agar-š čiš andar nēst ān rāy juttar.ēdōn paydāg kū ān

     pēš gōwešnīh padīriftārīh ēd i raftagīhā būd.ka-š.anda

     ān hangām.xwēdōdāh pad kunišn nē rāyēnēd.uš.pas.pad ha:

     kirbagīh-i ēn mārd.kē-š drahm awiš dād.be rāyēnēd.ān

     saxwan padīrišn i pēš raft būd rāy.ka gōwēd.ka-iz nē.

     ēg-š juttarīh ēd pad-š nēst.

4.   im xwēdōdāh.im kirbag rāyēnēd bawēd.ud rāyēnīdār ud

     drahm dādār āgenēn[1] ham-kirbag hēnd.ōy-šān har dōān

     kirbag-i xwēdōdāh warzišnīh bunīgīhā xwēš.

---

1.   Ank. reads <u>akvīn</u> .

Answer 22

3. If there is nothing else implied in this question
    which would require another answer, it is obvious that
    the former verbal acceptance is bygone, since in that
    period of time, xwēdōdāh actually was not carried out.
    Later on through joint benefaction of this man who had
    offered money, [xwēdōdāh] was exercised. [Therefore]
    the word of acceptance [of marriage] which was said
    before, be it mentioned or not, makes no difference.

4. This [performed] xwēdōdāh constitutes this meritorious
    deed. The one who carried it out and the one who gave
    money share the meritorious deed. Both of them
    will benefit from the entire benefaction of this
    xwēdōdāh.

pursišn 23

1. mard-ē kē zan-ē i čagar pad zanīh gīrēd.agar zan
    widarān bawēd.mard andar xwāstag-i zan kē-š būd.pēš
    az ān kū ō zanīh-i im mard mad.bahr bawēd ayāb nē.
    zan az mard bawēd ayāb nē.ud frazand kē-šān mayān
    zāyēd az xwāstag-i pidar čand.ud ān-i mādar čand.
    rasēd.agar mard az zan pad zanīh gīrēd.paymān nē
    kunēd ku-m az sīnag-masāy ud bāzā-masāy be hišt hēd.
    pas az čand sāl xwāhēd.pad xwāstan pādixšāy bawēd
    ayāb nē.agar pādixšā.čand rasēd.

Question 23

1. A man who marries a čagar[1] woman, if she dies, has this man any share regarding the property that belonged to her prior to her marriage to this man. Does the wife have any share of the husband's property [should he die first]?[2] The children who are born to them, how much would they inherit from their father's property and how much from their mother's. If the man takes the capital of the woman on the basis of her wifeship [i.e. belonging to him], but does not make any agreement that from what is remitted to him, he would take only sufficient amount to make both ends meet[3] [which is the minimum amount for curatorship of a capital in somebody's trust[4]], yet years later he claims it, would he be entitled to such a claim or not, and if so, how much goes over to him?

---

1. It would be appropriate to point out that the word čagar which is frequently used in this section, covers a wide range of meanings in Pahlavi texts such as: step mother or father, or son or daughter, collateral wife, a widow or widower, a girl who has no brother or father when she marries. Even a father who has children other than those by his main wife would be a čagar father. In short, it seems that most family relationships which are not original and are somehow substituted, fall in the category of čagar.

2. Although the present translation of this sentence is suggested by Dr. Bishop of Columbia University, I still believe the literal translation which would go as:"Does the woman belong to the man or not?"would be as correct, regarding the fact that a čagar woman belongs to the former husband in that world. R.HF., p. 195.

3. See note 1, tr., ans. 5, sec. 15.

4. See ans. 18, sec. 12.

passox 23

2. agar-š čiš andar nēst ān rāy juttar.hangirdīg ēn
    kū.pad ān i abāz ō xīr-i xwāstag.i-šan pad dārišn ud
    xwēšīh har dō ēstēd.girēd.

3. ēn ku xwāstag-i zan-i čagar ō šōy čagar.ān i šōy
    čagar ō zan-i čagar pad bē widarišn ēk az i-šan ō ōy
    did nē rāsēd.bē pad pašn hastišn bahr ud dād tā
    frārāst.

4. ka-šān frazand mayān bawēd.ān pašn hastišn juttarīh
    pad-š kam-iz nēst.ud frazand i-šān mayān zād.ān az
    abāz hišt ziyānag gīrēd.

5. ka ziyānag widarān.agar frazand ēk.hamāg ō ān ēk.
    agar pus.pad xwēšīh.ud agar duxt.pad ayōkēnīh.i mard
    i pādixšāīhā rasēd.

Answer 23

2. If there is nothing else implied in the question which would require another answer, a brief explanation would be the following: they are entitled to take the capital of each other.

3. The property of a čagar wife or a čagar husband does not go from one to the other if either one dies . But on existing conventions, a share and donation up to the amount of frarāst[1] can be given to either .

4. When children are born to them it makes not even the least difference to the existing convention. With regard to children born to them the temporary wife [ziyānag[2]] gets [her personal share] from what is left behind [by the deceased husband].[3]

5. If the temporary wife dies, if there is only one child [born to her], all [her property] goes to that one child. If that child is a boy, the property directly goes to his own possession. If a girl, it goes to the man who accepts her ayōkēnīh.[4]

---

1. One "cubit", W. H. Henning, "An Astronomical Chapter and Bundahišn", Journal of the Royal Asiatic Society, (London, 1942), p. 236.

2. See C.Bartholomae, NSL. (1936), XXX, 6.

3. See R.HF., p. 203.

4. See Question 1, note 4.

passox 23, cont'd.

6.　　agar wēš kū ēk pus duxt hēnd.and-čand hišt mādar.
　　　　mayān-šān pusīhā ud duxtīhā baxšišn.

7.　　agar pus ēk-iz nēst.duxt dō hast.ēk az i-šān
　　　　ayōkēnīh pid pādixšāihā.

8.　　bē agar ān i mēh nē xwāhēd.pad ān i kēh frāz hilēd.
　　　　andar ušān ān i mēh pad-š sazāgtar.

9.　　ud ayōkēnīh pad har kē az-i-šān be ēstēd.ayōkēnīh rāy.
　　　　az sē bahr dō bahr be stānēd.ān i did sē ēk-ē.

10.　　agar šōy nē kunēd.ud uš pid-iz čagar frāz rawēd.uš
　　　　stūr abāyēd gumārdan.

11.　　ēn duxt-i čagar pad sturīh pidar čagar sazāgtar.pad-š
　　　　be gumārišn.

Answer 23, cont'd.

6. If there are more than one girl or boy, what is left
   behind from their deceased mother should be distributed
   amongst them according to boy's and girl's share regulations.

7. If there are no boys but two girls, then one of the girls
   is entitled to the ayōkēnīh of her father.

8. But, if the older one does not want [her father's
   ayōkēnīh], then it goes [i.e. the right] to the younger
   one. [But] among them, the older one is more appropriate [for this ayōkēnīh].

9. Whichever one of the girls   becomes the ayōkēn [of
   the father] will have two shares out of three shares because of her ayōkēnīh. The other girl, one third.

10. If she does not marry and her widower father passes away,
    it would be necessary that a proxy be appointed for her.

11. This čagar girl [unmarried, fatherless and motherless] is
    the most suitable [person] to become her father's stūr[1].
    She should be assigned to that.

---

1. See Q. 18, note **2** .

pass̲o̲x̲ ̲2̲3̲, cont'd.

12. agar.pēš kū-š pidar i čagar be widarēd.šōy kūnēd.
pādixšā zan-i im šōy bawēd.pas pidar i čagar be frāz
rawēd.uš stūr abāyēd gumardan.ān duxt i šōy kardag.
nē rasēd.ud hišt-i pidar-i čagar.ēg-š xwēšrāyišn [1]
pad-š weh.

13. ēn pad-š nigerišn kū frazand az zan-i čagar pad pusarī
ud duxtīh padīrift ēstēd ayāb nē.ēn-iz kū-š zan frazand
pādixšāīhā hast ayāb nē.

14. čē.agar-š frazand az zan-i čagar.pus pad pusarīh ud
duxt pad duxtīh padīrift ēstēnd.uš zan ud frazand
padixšāīhā hast.baxšišn i-š abar xīr-ē xwāstag abar
frazandān pādixšāīhā.pus zan-iz i pādixšāīhā abāg-šān
ham-bahr čiyōn pus-ē.

---

1. Ank. reads a̲ū̲s̲r̲ā̲y̲i̲s̲n̲ . Perikhanian reads x̲w̲a̲s̲r̲ā̲y̲i̲š̲n̲.

swer 23, cont'd.

. If she marries before her widower father passes away,
she will be the pādixša wife of her husband. Later, when
her father passes away, a proxy should be appointed for
him. It [proxyhood] does not go to the married girl,
and the property left by the widower father, under the
circumstances, is best to be kept in "self entrusting"[2]
condition.

. This [fact] should be carefully examined: whether
[any] child of the collateral[3] wife has been adopted as
adopted son, or daughter or not. Also the fact [should
be examined] whether there is any main[4] wife and
children, or not.

. Because if any child of the collateral wife is being
adopted as son or daughter and there is also a main wife
and her children, all those children are entitled to a
share of that capital and property. Even the one who
has been adopted [inherits] according to the boy's-girl's
share. Also the son of the main wife inherits equal share
with them as though they were one.

See   Q. 1, note 1.

The latter part of this passage is confusing, unless it is compared
with ans. 18, sec.7. Also although Perikhanian in "Some Pahlavi
Legal Terms", Henning Mem. Vol. (London, 1970) p. 351 refers to this
particular occurence of this word in this passage while discussing
her point about xwāsrāy marriage, I think here the word does not
qualify the girl but the property.

See   C. Bartholomae, NSL., (1931), XVIII, 36.

See   pādixša wife, Q. 1, note 1, also Bartholomae, op. cit., p. 36.

passox 23, cont'd.

15. agar-š frazand az zan-i čagar.pus pad pusarīh.duxt
    pad duxtarīh.nē padīrift ēstēd.uš zan frazand pādixšāī
    hast.ō ān i čagar rāy nē rasēd.

16. ēg-š zan frazand pādixšāīhā nēst.ān-i az zan-i čagar.
    pus pad pusarīh duxt pad duxtarīh.padīrift ēstēd.
    pusīhā duxtīhā ō frazand zan i čagar rasēd.

17. agar-š frazand az zan-i čagar pad pusarīh ud duxtarīh
    nē padīrift ēstēd.ēg-š xwāstag hamāg pad stūrīh ēstēd.
    ēk-ē az frazandān-i az zan-i čagar pad-š sazāgtar.ud
    ka hamāg ēwdom hēnd wizēn-i pad-š fradom pad pus-i
    mēh pad sturīh-i pid-i čagar be gumārišn.uš hamāg
    xwāstag-i pid-i čagar pad rāh-i stūrīh be awiš rasēd.

18. agar ān i mēh pad sturīh nē šāyēd.any pus hast šāyēd.
    bē ō ān i pas az ān i mehtar rasēd pad stūrīh gumārdagī

Answer 23, cont'd.

15. If any child of the collateral wife has not been
     adopted as son and daughter and there is also a main
     wife with her children, [the inheritance]does not go
     to that [i.e. the unadopted children] of the collateral
     wife.

16. If [he had] no main wife and children, [the inheritance]
     goes to the children of the collateral wife who have
     been adopted as sons and daughters, on the basis of legal
     boy's-girl's portion.

17. If the children of the collateral wife have not been
     adopted as sons and daughters, then all the property
     will remain in curatory[1]. One of the children of the
     collateral wife would be more deserving of it. If all
     of them [the children] are at similar conditions, then
     priority of being elected goes to the eldest son. He
     should be assigned as the curator of the čagar father.
     [Therefore] all the property of the [deceased] čagar fa-
     ther will be handed over to him, by way of curatorship.

18. If the eldest son is not suitable for curation, and
     there is another son, the office should go over to the
     one who is next oldest.

---

1.   stūrīh, see C. Bartholomae, NSL., (1936), XXX, 70.

passox 23, cont'd.

19. agar pus nēst.ayāb ān i hast pad stūrīh nē šāyēd.
     duxt ēčand hēnd.az i-šān ēk ayōkēnīh ud sturīh pidar-i
     čagar.ud pad-š be gumārišn.

20. uš xwāstag-i pidar-i čagar hamāg pad rāh-i stūrīh-i
     pidar-i čagar be awiš rasēd.stūr dūdag kadag bānūg-i
     pidar-i čagar bawēd.·

21. agar az zan čagar ēwāz ēk duxt hast.ēg saxwan pad-š
     dō ēwēnag.ēk ān i ka-š mādar zīndag.ēk ān i ka-š
     mādar nē zīndag.

22. čē agar-š mādar zīndag ān ēk duxt ēg-š ayōkēnīh ud
     sturīh-i pidar-i čagar gumārdagīhā be awiš rasēd.
     abāg hamāg xwāstag-i pidar-i čagar.

23. ud pas.ka-š pidar frāz rawēd.uš any frazand pad jud
     az ēn duxt-ē kē pad ayōkēnīh sturīh pidar-i čagar
     gumārd ēstēd.nēst.xwāstag im zan be hilēd.pad sturīh
     i-š šōy pādixšāīhā ēstēd.ō ōy rawēd kē andar dudag i
     ōy nazdīk paywandīgtar ud sazāgtar.

Answer 23, cont'd.

19. If there is no son, or if the existing one does not
     deserve the job, and there are girls [instead], one
     of them should be designated as ayōkēn and proxy for
     her čagar father.

20. In that case all the property of her čagar father goes
     over to her by way of curatorship. She will become
     proxy of the family and the lady of the household of
     her [deceased] čagar father.

21. If there is only one girl from the collateral wife,
     the procedure[1] would be of two sorts. One, when the
     mother is [still] alive. The other one, when she is
     no longer alive.

22. Because if the mother is alive, then the ayōkēnīh and
     curatorship of the čagar father goes to her [i.e. the
     girl].

23. Afterwards, when the father passes away, and he has no
     other child except that girl who has been assigned for
     his ayōkēnīh and curatorship, the property he leaves
     for this woman would go to the curatorship of the hus-
     band [whom she would marry] lawfully. [That is] it
     goes to the person [man] who is nearest in relation [to
     her] and is most eligible.

---

1.   saxwan, in addition to its common meaning, often means legal pro-
     cedure in judicial terms. See C.Bartholomea, NSL.,(1967),XLI,22-5.

171

24. ud agar mādar-i im duxt nē zindag.im ēk duxt ayōkēn-i
pidar i pādixšāīhā bawēd.uš xwāstag-i mādar hamāg bē
awiš rasēd.sturīh-i pid-i čagar be ō ōy rasēd kē-š
andar dūdag nabānazdištar.

25. agar-š ēn duxt-i zan-i čagar pad duxtarīh padirift
ēstēd.uš xwāstg wēš kū xwāstag-i sturīh kamīh ēd andar
nē āyēd.

26. ud agar mād hēšt ēstēd wēš kū xwāstag-i stūrīh ē nēst
im xwāstag hamāg be ō sturīh šawēd.ō duxt čiš-iz nē
rasēd.

27. agar im xwāstag wēš kū stūrīh ēd hast.ān i wēš ud kam
kū bahr-i duxt-i be ō duxt dahišn.

28. agar wēš kū bahr-i duxt.bahr-i duxt duxtīhā bē dahišn.
abārīg abar xwāstag-i stūrīh be abzāyišn.

Answer 23, cont'd.

24. If the mother of this girl is not alive, the girl is
    legally under ayōkēnĭh of her father, and all the property
    of the mother goes to her. [But] the curatorship of
    the căgar father goes to the person who is the nearest
    relative in the family.

25. If the daughter of the collateral wife had been adopted
    as an adopted daughter and the property is more than
    the [minimum amount of] property which should go in
    trust[1], no reduction should be made to it.

26. If what the mother has left is not more than the "amount
    in trust", all of it goes to trust and will not be
    handed over to the girl.

27. If it is more than the amount in trust from that excess,
    that which is in excess and is less than the daughter's
    portion should be given to the daughter.

28. If [that extra] is more than the legal girl's portion,
    the share of the daughter should be remitted and what
    remains should be added to the amount which is in trust.

---

1. See ans. 18, sec. 7.

passox 23, cont'd.

29.   ān-i sinag-masāy ud bāzā-masāy rāy nibišt.kē-š nē hišt ēstēd.hamē ka-š abāyēd pādixšāīhā xwāst stānēd.

30.   andāzag ān sinag-masāy bāzā-masāy pad rāh-i dudagsālārᵢ ān-īz i sturīh-i dēnīg. har rōz šabān rāy.sē panj ēk-i drahm-ē purr.az-š[1] wastargān wahāg-iz pad-š dūdagsālārᵢ dēnīg.ēg-š ēdōn ast[-ē][2] xwēšīh ast[-ē][3] kaš kār-i dūdagsālārīh dēnīgīhā rāyēnēd.

_____

1.   Ank. reads uš.

2.   Ank. reads hast. see tr. same sec., note 2.

3.   Ank. amends to ēdōn. MS. ast.

Answer 23, cont'd.

29. As for that [least] sufficient amount [for curation]
to make both ends meet, which has been already discussed[1],
should it not be remitted, it is lawful to ask for and
receive it.

30. The lawful proportion of that least sufficient amount
[for curation], regarding family guardianship, as
well as that of curatorship is 3/5th of a drahm daily,
from which clothing expenses of the family guardian is
legally [supplied]. So, in this way, a portion[2] goes to
the possession of the family itself and a portion goes
to the person who has fulfilled the task of family
guardianship legally.

---

1. See ans. 5, sec. 15.

2. ast-ē Bartholomae, in legal terms renders it as "partly". See
C. Bartholomae , NSL., (1936),XXX,31.

175

pursišn 24

1. mard-ē.kē-š xwahar-ē bawēd.az pidar ud mādar.pad

   hamdādestānīh-i xwahar. frāz padīrēd.kū.xwahar pad

   zanīh gīrēm.[1]ud pēš az ān ku gugāy abar gīrēd.uš be

   sālārīh rasēd.mard-ē rasēd.uš abēdastwarīh-i pidar

   mādar ud brādar.pad zanīh gīrēd.uš wināhkārīh tā čē

   sāmānag.

---

1. Ank. reads <u>kunōm</u>

Question 24

1. [assume] A man who has a sister from [his own] father
    and mother, with the consent of his sister   agrees to
    take her as his wife. [But] before making it official,
    and before [his] becoming a family authority, a man
    comes and without the representation[1] of father, mother,
    and brother, marries her. What is the proportion of
    his sinfulness?

---

1. dastwarīh apart from its common meaning, in judicial terms equals
    yātakgōw meaning representative. See C. Bartholomae, NSL. (1967)
    XLI, 93.

passox 24

2. agar-š čiš andar nēst ān rāy juttar; wināh i pad ēn
ēwēnag andar pāyag-i zan apparīh.ud zan apparīh andar
pāyag-i margarzānīh.uš ēn-iz andar kū grān wināh-i
xwēdōdāh škenišnīh pad-š

3. andar weh dēn.ēdōn paydāg.kū.kē xwēdōdāh ēd be škenēd.
ōwōn ku ān xwēdōdāh ō kardan nē āyēd.ēg-š ō ān i pāhlom
axwān nē rasēd.mayān ōy ud pāhlom axwān tanišn-ē čand
zamīg pahnāy ud zofāy be ēstēd.uš ō ān-i pāhlom axwān
nē helēnd.

Answer 24

2. If there is nothing else implied in the question which
    would require another answer, the level of such a sin
    equals the level of wife-kidnapping (adultery). The
    level of wife-kidnapping sin is death. In his case, the
    grave sin of breaking a next-of-kin marriage is also
    [added].

3. In Zoroastrian religion, it is so declared that he who
    breaks a next-of-kin marriage in such a way that marriage
    never takes place, he [the breaker] will never get to the
    best existence [Heaven]. Between him and the best exis-
    tence there would be a distance as wide and as deep as
    that of the earth. He would not be allowed into the best
    existence.

pursišn 25

1.   mard-ē.kē az dād-i weh-dēn ō dād-i akdēnīh šawēd.

xwāstag čiš andar weh dēnīh būd.pad-š akdēnīh bawēd

ayāb nē.agar kas stānēd.pādixšā ayāb nē.ud agar nē

pādixšā.kū abāyēd burdan.

Question 25

1. A man who changes his religion from Zoroastrian to Islam[1], does the property which he owned in his Zoroastrian faith belong to him now that he has become a Moslem? If some one seizes that property, would it be lawful? If not, where should it be taken?

---

1. See Men. "La Rivāyat d.Emēt Ašavahištān." <u>Revue de l'Histoire des Religion</u> (Presses Universitaire de France, Paris, 1962), p. 76; also H.K. Mirza , appendix question 1.

passox 25

2. agar-š čiš andar nēst ān rāy juttar.kas-ē kē dād
   wehdēnīh ō dād akdēnīh šawēd.zamānīg pad gyāg tanāpuhl
   wināh.

3. ka.andar sāl dranāy.abāz ō wehdēnīh nē āyēd.pas az
   sāl dranāy margarzān.

4. uš xir ud xwāstag-ē pad xwēšīh ēstēd ud windišn-iz
   kē-š pad weh dēnīh xwēš būd.pad paoiryāi dāmanạm
   ēstēd.

5. Paoiryāi dāmanạm.kē.

6. ka ēn kū har kē az weh dēnān ān xir ud xwāstag fradom
   abar gīrēd.pad xwēšīh-i xwēš dārēd.pādixšā.

7. agar-š andar dārišn tuwān kū abāz ō akdēn nē dahēd.
   pad xwēšīh dāstan pādīxšā.

8. agar-š nē tuwān kū pad xwēš dārēd.ō ōy dahēd kē.ka weh
   dēn būd.a-š xwēš būd.

Answer 25

2. If there is nothing else implied in this question which
    would require another answer, he who changes his reli-
    gion from Zoroastrianism to Islam, has committed a
    tanāpuhl sin at that very moment.

3. If within the period of a year he does not go back to
    Zoroastrianism, when the year expires he deserves death.

4. Any property, wealth or income that belonged to him
    while he was Zoroastrian, becomes subject to the "Law
    of Primitive Men".

5. The "Law of Primitive Men" is that:

6. Any Zoroastrian who seizes that property first, is en-
    titled to possess it.

7. If it is possible to keep it and not give it back to
    the Moslem, he [the seizor] is permitted to keep it.

8. If he is not capable of keeping it for himself, he must
    return it to the person to whom it belonged while he
    was a Zoroastrian.

183

pursišn 26

1. mard-ē kē pad ō akdēnīh rasēd.pas pašēmān bawēd.pad

   petīt bawēd.kirbag warzīdārīh ēd kunēd.pas az widardagī▮

   ruwān abāyēd yaštan ayāb nē.ud agar xwad pad akdēnīh

   zāyēd.kirbag warzīdār ud pad weh dēn ēstēd.uš dādestān

   čē.ud dahīšn ahlawdād abāyēd dādan ayāb nē.

Question 26

. [Assume] a Zoroastrian has become a Moslem. Later he
is regretful and repents and performs some meritorious
deed. After his passing away, should the ceremonial rite
for veneration of the soul be offered to him or not?
If he is born a Moslem [but] performs all the benefactions and becomes a Zoroastrian, what would be the religious declaration? Should the charity donation (ahlawdād)
for the priest be given or not?

<u>passox 26</u>

2. agar-š čiš andar nēst ān rāy juttar.kē andar sāl dranāy
pašēmān.pad petīt bawēd.kirbag.andar weh dēn kirbag.tuw
sāmānīhā.warzēd.az wināh.andar weh dēn pad wināh.tuwān
sāmānīhā pahrēzēd.ka widarān bawēd.ēg-š ruwān.čiyōn ān
wehdēnān.yaštan abāyēd.

3. agar.pas az sāl dranāy.pad petīt bawēd.kirbag warzīdār
ud az wināh pahrēzdār.pad ān ēwēnag kū abar nibišt.anda
astišnīh im ēwēnag petītīgīh widarēd.ēg-š petītīgīh rāy
rūwan az dušox bōzihēd.čē.petītīgīh be rāh i ō dušox nē

4. uš.rōz-i čahārum stōš bun kunišn.abārīg čiyōn ān i weh
dēnān.

5. hamē ka pad petītīgīh az āwām šawēd.kirbag wināh ī-š ka
ēstēd hamāg pad stōš hamāl pad-š bawēd.

Answer 26

2. If there is nothing else implied in the question which
would require another answer, he who regrets within a year
and repents and performs within his possibilities the
meritorious deeds which are advocated in Zoroastrianism
and avoids as much as possible sins which are recognized
in Zoroastrianism, then when he dies the rite of soul
worshipping should be offered to him just as it would be
offered to a Zoroastrian.

3. If after a year, he repents and performs meritorious deeds
and avoids committing sins, [he should be treated] as mentioned above. If he thus repents while still alive, because of his repentence his soul would be redeemed from
hell because repentance is not the way of perdition.

4. On the fourth day the rite of stōš[1] as well as other ceremonies as advocated in the Zoroastrian religion should be
offered for his soul.

5. As long as he passes away repentant, his benefactions
would balance out his sins on the occasion of stōš.

---

1. The fourth morning after death when it is believed that the judgement of the man's deeds takes place. Therefore, imploring God's
blessings and mercy by the relatives and friends of the deceased on
this particular occasion is considered a benefaction. See J.Modi,
Religious Ceremonies and Customs of the Parsees, (Bombay, 1922),p.84.

187

passox 26, cont'd.

6.   ka-š pad stōš tōzišn ud pādifrāh wizārd.gyāg ān-š ruwān
pad mēnōgān.čiyōn-š az kirbag warzišnīh xwēšīnēd ēstēd.
pad hammistagān pāyag ayāb abartar.

7.   ud ān-i hamgōnag.ka andar stōš be ō saxtīh rasēd.ēg-š
tišn ud suy ud sarmāg ud garmāg az-š abāz dāštan
frēzbānīg.ud ka nē kunēnd.[1] wināh.

8.   ud abāz-iz.akdēnān kē-šān akdēnīh az abarmānd.ne az
xwadīh āškārāg akdēnān kard ud šud hēnd.ud hamē ka ēr
barišnīh az wīnāh.i andar weh dēn wināh.pahrēzēd.kirbag
i pad weh dēn kirbag.tuwān sāmānīhā warzēd.pad-iz dahiš
ahlawdād čimīg ud nē wināh.

---

1.   Ank. reads <u>kunēd</u>.

Answer 26, cont'd.

5.   When on st$\bar{o}\check{s}$ his atonement and retributions are fulfilled, his soul would be at the place of heavenly creatures, since ($\check{c}$iy$\bar{o}$n) his performance of benefactions [elevated him] to the level of hammistag$\bar{a}$n[1] or even higher.

7.   Thus a person who goes through the hardship of the [ordeal] of st$\bar{o}\check{s}$, it is a religious duty to unburden him from the thirst, hunger, cold and heat [which he had gone through]. If they [those who are alive] do not do it, [unburdening him by means of performing the rite of soul worshipping] it would be a sin.

8.   Further, he whose being a Moslem is through heritage and not by his own deliberate confession, as long as through noble behavior he avoids the sins which are recognized in Zoroastrianism, and performs benefactions that are advocated in Zoroastrianism within his possibilities, it would be proper to give [on his behalf] the charity donations of the priests. It would not be a sin.

---

1.   Neutral station between heaven and hell.

pursišn 27

1.   mard-ē.kē pad drahm xwēdōdāh framāyēd.kirbag ān rāy
hamē kunēd.ud agar ēdōn kū har dō bawēd.paydāgēnēd
kū ēk ēk kirbag čand.

Question 27

1. If a man performs <u>xwēdōdāh</u> in terms of being paid
    for that, would the benefaction belong to the person
    who has offered the money, or to the person who has
    physically performed it? If the benefaction belongs
    to both of them, please clarify how much would be the
    share of each one.

<u>passox 27</u>

2. agar-š čiš andar nēst ān rāy juttar.ka ōy kē xwēdōdāh
    hamē.pad hamkirbagīh-i ōy kē drahm dahēd.rāyēnēd.ēg-šān
    xwēdōdāh har dō hast ēwdom rāst.bē.ōy kē xwēdōdāh pad
    tan-i xwēš rāyēnēd ēstēd.pad mēnōgān frāyīh-ē hast.i
    ōy rāy.kē pad tan-i xwēš nē kard ēstēd.nēst.

3. ēn hast.kū agar wahištīg.ēg-š ruwān gāh wuzurgīhātār.ud
    agar dušoxīg.ēg-š ruwān mēnōg xwēdōdāh pīm ud hanbasānī
    dušox az-š abāz dārēd.čiyōn frasp-ē ud drubuštīh i
    pērāmōn ruwān-i ān kē xwēdōdāh pad tan-i xwēš warzēd
    bawēd.

4. agar xēwōdāh nē pad hamkirbagīh ōy kunēd drahm dādār ba
    ōy i drahm dādār kirbag kam bawēd kū ōy i xwēdōdāh
    rāyēnīdār.

---

1. BTF. ‿⌣ ﺑﻮﺟﺎﺭ Ank. reads <u>akhvasih</u>. I think it is corrupted
    form of <u>hanbasānīh</u>. As for the 6 <u>m</u> in this word, in later Pahla-
    pronounciation <u>m</u> is changed to <u>n</u>, eg. the very word in MK. which
    he reads <u>m</u> with the spelling <u>n</u>. See plate.

Answer 27

2. If there is nothing else implied in the question which
would require another answer, when a person performs
the xwēdōdāh on the basis of joint benefaction with the
person who paid for it, then their share in the benefaction is exactly equal. But, he who has performed it
physically has extra [privileges] in heaven, he who has
not performed it physically, has not [those extra
privileges].

3. It is certain that if [he who performed it is supposed
to be] heavenly, then his place of soul would be higher
and if [he is] hellish, then the spirit of xwēdōdāh
would keep him away from the misery and conflicts of
hell. [The good deed] will function as a wall or for-
tress surrounding the soul of the person who had performed xwēdōdāh with his own body [physically].

. If xwēdōdāh is not based on joint benefaction[1] with the
person who has given the money, then the benefaction of
the person who has provided the money would be less than
that of the person who has executed it.

. Perhaps by not hamkirbagīh, it is meant that while helping financially it is not meant to be spent on xwēdōdāh, but ultimately it
is used for that purpose.

pursišn 28

1. xwēdōdāh kē abāg mādar ud xwahar kunēd.kē-šān ēmēd-i
    frazand zāyišn az-š nēst.kirbag-i xwēdōdāh bowandag baw?
    ayāb čiyōn.kirbag-i xwēdōdāh hamāg ēk ayāb ast-ē wēš
    kirbagtar.

Question 28

1. If xwēdōdāh is with a mother or a sister for whom there is no hope of producing any children, would it be [considered] a perfect xwēdōdāh or how [would it be considered]? Is the merit of all xwēdōdāh-s the same or are some (ast-ē[1]) more meritorious [than others]?

---

1. See ans. 23, note 2, sec. 30.

passox 28

2. xwēdōdāh.abāg har sē.pad har dād i hēnd.ka kunēnd.
    kirbag-i xwēdōdāh bowandagīhā.ud ēd rāy ka-š frazand
    az-š nē bawēd kamīh-ē abar kirbag-i xwēdōdāh andar nē
    āyēd.

Answer 28

1. xwēdōdāh with any one of the three,[1] whatever age they
   are, is [considered] a perfect xwēdōdāh. For this reason if there is no child, the benefaction of xwēdōdāh
   would not decrease.

---

1. The figure three might suggest mother, sister, daughter. (tr.'s note).

197

pursišn 29

1. kē xwēdōdāh kunēd.i uš az xwēdōdāhīh kūn-marzīhēd
ēg-iz kunēd.ēg-š dādestān čē.kē-š pēš kūn-marz kard
bawēd.pas xwēdōdāh.dādestān čē.

Question 29

1. He who undertakes xwēdōdāh, then from xwēdōdāh turns

    into practicing sodomy, then again practices [xwēdōdāh];

    what would be the religious judgement? He who had prac-

    ticed sodomy before and later [performed] xwēdōdāh, what

    would be the religious judgement [in this case]?

passox 29

2. har kē kūn-marz kunēd margarzān.

3. ēn wināh ōwōn grān kū-š kirbag-iz-i xwēdōdāh az-š
    appār be kunēd.

4. bē agar pēš radān māndag griyēd menīšnīhā az im wināh
    pad petīt bawēd.tan ō pādifrāh-i tōzišn abespārēd.
    agar-š pad sar pādifrāh gīrēd.ēg-š gētīgīha wizārd.

5. agar nē.az gētīg apetītīgīhā be šawēd.ēg-š pad mēnōgān
    az xwēdōdāh pad tan-i xwēš warzišnīh.ān ēwēnag ēd sūd
    bawēd. čiyōn ōy i xwēdōdāh pad tan-i xwēš warzidār ēst
    rāy andar dušox.

6. ka andar gētīg pad petīt bawēd.uš nē ozanēnd.petītīgīh
    az āwām šawēd.ēg-š pad stōš āmār tōzišn abar kunēnd.[1]

7. ka-š pad stōš wizārd.ēg-š hamāg kirbag abāg-iz ān-i
    xwēdōdāh abāz awiš dahēnd.

---

1. Ank. reads kūnēt.

Answer 29

2. Whoever commits sodomy deserves margarzān.

3. This sin is so grave that it even nullifies the merits of xwēdōdāh.

4. But if [the sinner] laments in the presence of a high priest and with all his heart repents from this sin and submits his body to retribution for redemption; if his retribution reaches its uttermost[1] (pad sar), then he will be redeemed in this corporeal world.

5. If he passes away from this world not repentant, then in the spiritual world, on account of his physical practice of xwēdōdāh, he would have the same privilege as he who is protected in hell because of his physical xwēdōdāh practice.

6. If he repents in this world, and is not killed [not gone through margarzān], and passes away repentant, then on the day of stōš his atonement would be considered.

7. If he is redeemed at [the ordeal of] stōš, then all his meritorious deeds along with that of his xwēdōdāh will be given back to him.

---

1. Men. "La Rīvāyāt D'Ēmēt I Ašavahištān", Revue de l'Histoire des Religions, (Presses Universitaires de France, Paris 1962), p.86 translates "si on recoit le châtiment (en payant) de sa tête (pat sar)".

passox 29, cont'd.

8.   kūn-marz.wĕš grāyīh   rāy.ēd i pĕš ēd i pas ēwdom.

Answer 29, cont'd.

8.   Sodomy, because of its extreme grievousness, whether

practiced before or after [xwēdōdāh] would be the same.

pursišn 30

1. mard-ē kē-š menišn pad xwēdōdāh bawēd.ān kē-š abāg
    āyēd kardan pad wistarag dārēd.pad kāmag wizardan
    atuwānīg.dādmēh ayāb wēmārīh rāy.ēg-š kirbag-i
    xwēdōdāh bawēd ayāb nē.

Question 30

1. A man who has the intention of xwēdōdāh goes to bed
   with whom he can consummate [the] marriage. He is
   unable to fulfil the desire, either because of old age
   or because of [some] illness. Under these circumstances,
   would it be [considered] the benefaction of xwēdōdāh
   or not?

passox 30

2.   kirbag-i xwēdōdāh ēdōn bawēd.ka-iz pad kunišn kard.ka-

menišnīhā.uš kardan nē tuwān.ka-iz atuwānīgīh rāy.ō

kardan nē rasēd ān-iz kirbag.i pad kunīšn bowandagīhā

kunīhēd.nē pad kard hangārišn.bē-š ēg-iz menišnīgīhā

rāy.wuzurg ruwān frayād ō bawēd.

Answer 30

2.   The merit of xwēdōdāh holds whether by actual performance, or [merely] by intention which can never be
fulfilled. If due to impotency it cannot be carried
out, still it is [considered] a benefaction. That
[xwēdōdāh] which is not completely done cannot be considered an accomplished one, but because of the [meri-
torious] intention, it would be a great relief for the
soul.

pursišn 31

1. mard-ē kē zan-ē čagar pad zanīh gīrēd.nē dānēd.ēg-š
wināh bawēd ayāb nē.ud agar-š bawēd.čand bawēd.

2. duxt-i ayōkēn kadār.ud ān-i bayaspān kadār.

Question 31

1. A man who takes a čagar woman as a wife and is unaware
   of her being a čagar; has he committed a sin or not?
   If so, what would be the proportion of his sin?

2. Who is an ayōkēn daughter? and who is a bayaspān.[1]

---

1. According to A. Perikhanian the word bayaspān is another version of
   "xwāsrāy marriage" both of which designate self-guardianship, full
   right marriage. See A. Perikhanian, "On Some Pahlavi Legal Terms",
   W.B. Henning Mem. Vol., (London, 1970), pp. 349-51.

passox 31

3. agar im mard ēn zan-i čagar pad čagarīh zanīh zan kunēd
xūb.wināh-ē nē bawēd.agar juttar.zan kardan kār-ē hast
frašgirdīg.pad čimtar abāyēd kardan.ud dō ēwēnag bawēd.
ēk pādixšā ud ēk čagar.

4. ōy kē zan-ē pad zanīh kāmēd kardan pēš az zan kardan.
az zan āgāh be abāyēd būdan kū pādīxšā zan hast ayāb
čagar.

5. ud ka-iz ēd āgāhīhā zan kunēd.eg-š zanīh nē xūb kard
bawēd.ō frazand ō ruwān-iz wizāyišnīg.

6. čē.agar čagar hast ud dānēd kū čagar.uš pad pādixšāzanīhā
zanīh dārēd.pad gyāg tanāpuhl.ud pad sāl dranāy margarzār

7. agar pādixšāīhā.uš pad čagar zanīh gīrēd dārēd.ān zanīh
ud šōyīh nē xūb.wišōbišnīg abāyišn.

Answer 31

3. It would be all right if this man under the conditions
    of čagar wifeship takes this woman as his wife. There
    is no sin in it. On the other hand, taking a wife is
    [supposed to be] a matter lasting to the Renovation. It
    should be carried out with full consideration. And there
    are two kinds of it [wifeship]. One pādixšā,[1] the other
    one čagar.[2]

4. He who desires to take a woman as a wife, before taking
    her, he must make sure whether she is a pādixšā or a
    čagar.

5. Even if he marries with this information and then the
    marriage does not come out as desired, it would be an
    injury to the children as well as to the soul.

6. Because, if she is a čagar and [he] knows that, and yet
    keeps her as a pādixšā wife, he has committed a tanāpuhl
    sin at that very moment, a sin which would become
    margarzān within a year.

7. If she is a pādīxšā wife and he keeps her as a čagar, that
    would not be a proper marriage, it should be broken.

---

1. See Q. 1, note 1, also Bartholomae, NSL, (1931), XVIII, 36.
2. See ans. 1, note 3, also Bartholomae, op. cit., p. 36.

passox 31, cont'd.

8. duxt-i ayōkēn ān bawēd.ka mard frāz rawēd.uš zan
    pādixšāīhā nēst.ēwāz duxt ēd hast.ān duxt ēd ayōkēn-i
    pidar.

9. agar xwahar.kē brād ēd.brād frāz rawēd.uš zan ud
    frazand pādixšāīhā pus-i padīriftag ud stūr kardag nēst.
    ēwāz ēn xwahar ēd hast.ayōkēn brād bawēd.

10. ēd ān duxt bayaspān čand ēwēnag bawēd.

11. ēd ēwēnag.ka pid duxt ayāb brād xwahar-ē pad pādixšā
    zanīh.be ō mard-ē dahēd.uš be xānag-i šōy āyēd.ka im
    duxt az xānag-i pid.ayāb im xwahar az xānag-i brād.ō
    xānag-i šōy šawēd.bayaspān bawēd.

12. ēwēnag ēd.ān ka.duxt-ē ayāb xwahar-ē.abēdastwarīhā-i
    pid brād.pas az pānzdah-sālagīh.xwad kāmagīhā.az xānag-i
    pid ud brad bērōn šawēd.hamē gādār gīrēd.pid ayāb brād
    jutdādestānīh.pahikār pad-š nē kunēd.ka ō nazdīk-i gādār
    šawēd bayaspān bawēd.

Answer 31, cont'd.

8. An ayōkēn daughter is she who when a man [father] dies
    and has no pādixšā wife leaves only this one daughter.
    Then she becomes ayōkēn of her father.

9. If there is a sister whose brother has passed away and
    he had no main[1] wife and children nor an adopted son nor
    a provided[2] proxy and his only sister is she, then she
    becomes ayōkēn of this brother.

10. There are various types of bayaspān daughter.

11. One is this; when a father gives his daughter to a
    man as a main wife, or when a brother gives his sister
    to a man as a main wife and she goes to the house of
    that husband. When this girl leaves her father's house
    for her husband's or, when the sister leaves the brother's
    house for her husband's, she is a bayaspān.

12. Another type is this; when this daughter or sister
    without the consent of her father or brother, after the
    age of fifteen, goes out by her own wishes and finds a
    lover. The father and brother [though] disagreeing,[yet]
    do not detain her. When she goes to her lover she is a
    bayaspān.

---

1. C. Bartholomae, NSL., (1931) XVIII, 36.

2. See ans. 1, N.B.

passox 31, cont'd.

13. ēwēnag ēd.ān-i ka akāmagīhā pid ud brād bērōn šawēd.
    pid brād.az ō bērōn šudan windēdan nē tuwān.ka bērōn
    šawēd.uš gādār gīrēd.bayaspān bawēd. ēn-iz ēdōn bawēd
    čiyōn ka pānzdah sālag bawēd.

14. ēwēnag ēd.ān-i ka pānzdah sālag bawēd.uš šōy abāyēd.
    uš pid brād awiš ō šōy nē dahēnd.pad nē dādan andar-š
    wināhkār bawēnd.ud pas gādār ēd frāz gīrēd.bayaspān.
    bawēd.

214
__Answer 31__, cont'd.

13. Another type is this: she who leaves against the desires of her father or brother. [But] this father or brother are not able to prevent her, then when she goes out and takes a lover, she is a __bayaspān__.

14. Another type is she who is at the age of fifteen and must have a husband. [But] her father or brother have not given her to a husband. By not giving her to a husband they are already sinful, and when she takes a lover, she is a __bayaspān__.

pursišn 32

1. zan-ē.kē nasā bawēd pēš az čehel rōz.pāk bawēd. pādixšā
ka be šōyēd.agar.pēš az čehel rōz.be šōyēd.pas az šustar
gumānīg˙ bawēd.ēg-š dādestān čē.

Question 32

. A woman who is [polluted] with discharge of bodily[1]

refuse, would she be clean before forty days? Would

it be permissible if she washes [has ablution]? If

she receives ablution before forty days, [but] after

ablution becomes doubtful, what would be the religious

prescription?

---

1. i.e. who has given birth to a child. K.J. "Further to Ēmēt-i
Ašavahištan,"Münchener Studien zur Sprachwissenchaft, (München, 1972),
Heft 30, p. 72.

passox 32

2. pad-š nigerēd.zan-i nasā.pas az sē rōz-i naxust.andar
ham rōz naxust.hamē ka pāk bawēd.pādixšā šustan.

3. pas az šustan.andar dwāzdah rōz.ka-š čiš-ē az tan be
āyēd.agar ēwar paydāg kū nē az nasā.ēg-š pad pēšag abāz
šōyišn.

4. pas az dwāzdah rōz ka-š čiš-ē az tan be āyēd.bē ka ēwar
paydāg kū az nasā.ēg-š.nē pad nasā bē pad dastān.dārišn
bē ka ēwar paydāg kū nē pad dastān.pad any wēmārīh
dārišn.i-š pahrēz-i az-š naxust abāyēd.

Answer 32

. Bear in mind that a [polluted] woman with a discharge of
bodily refuse, after the first three days, or [even] on
that same first day, whenever she becomes clean [i.e.
bleeding and discharge stops] washing [herself] is permissible.

. After washing, within twelve days if anything exudes from
her body, if it is evident that [the discharge]
is not lochia, then she should receive professional[1] ablution once more.

. If after twelve days, [still] there is bodily discharge
other than obvious lochia, then it should not be regarded
as lochia, but as menstruation. If it proves to be other
than menstruation, then it is evident that it is neither
lochia nor menstruation. It should be considered as a-
nother disease for which the first [step] is to observe
precaution.

. ᵗᵉⁿⁿⁱ K.J. op. cit., p. 66 reads pixāk and translates "she
shall receive ablution with the stick,"and gives references for his
reading. Also see transl. sec. 7. ans. 19

pursišn 33

1. zan daštān.kē-š nō rōz az daštān šud būd.pāk be bawēd.
    tāig abāyed-š gīrft āyāb nē.ud šāyēd ka be šōyēd ud tāi
    nē gīrēd.jāmag-i daštānīg.pēš kū wārān bawēd.abganēd.
    nigerīšnīgīhā uš wārān pad-š be āyēd.šāyēd ayāb nē.agar
    šāyēd.pas be dastšōy abāyēd kardan ayāb nē.

Question 33

1. A menstruous woman for whom nine days have passed from [the start] of her menstruation becomes clean. Should she wait for tāig[1] or not? Would it be permissible that she receives ablution and not wait for tāig? Leaving menstruation clothing [outside] unsheltered (nigerišnigīha) prior to rainfall and later on rain falls upon it, would that be permissible or not? If yes, should the rite of dastšōy[2] be carried out afterwards or not?

---

1. پرسج seems to be a term relating to a precautional extra day allowed before ablution so that there would be no doubt regarding later menstrual flow. Although I could not find a definition for this word in any of the sources at my disposal, this seems to be the meaning suggested by the contexts. (tr's note)

2. Ceremony of washing with cattle urine. See R.HF., pp. 211-18.

passox 33

2. zan az nazdist rōz ka-š daštān nišast.pas az nō rōz
šabān.hamē ka pāk bawēd.zamānīg be pādixšā šustan.

3. pas az nō rōz šabān.ka nōg daštān bawēd.tāīg nē abāyēd
griftan.

4. jāmag-i daštānīg.ka xōnīh ud hixrōmandīh nasā-ē paydāg
pad-š nēst.peš az wārān.pad gyāg-ē i hušk ud xānagīg
nigerēd.

5. ka wārān ēdōn pad-š be bawēd hamāg be xwēsēd ud tar be
bawēd.šāyēd.

6. uš dastšōy nē abāyēd.pad āb-i xānīg ud rōdīg be pādīxšā
šustan.

7. agar gabāg ō wārān abganēd.nē šāyēd.wināh pad-š.čē tōg
i azērēn ēdōn bawēd čiyōn ka-š āb awīš rasēd.

Answer 33

2. After nine days and nights from the first day when a
    woman confines herself to her menstruation enclosure[1]
    (daštān nišastan) when she becomes clean [no more menses
    flow] it is the time for proper washing [ablution].

3. When nine days and nights have passed from her recent
    menstruation, there is no need for tāig waiting.

4. Menstruation clothing which is not stained with blood
    or excrement or discharges should be taken to a dry spot
    inside the house before it starts raining.

5. If rain falls on them and they become saturated and
    wet, it is permissible.

6. In that case they need not undergo the dastsōy washing.
    They should be washed properly with spring or river water.

.   It is not permissible to expose [menstruation] garments
    to rain. It is a sin. Because the bottom part [facing
    the ground] would be in a position that water would get
    into it.

---

1. "In menstruation, she is to be so seated that there should be fifteen
    steps of three feet each from the water apart from her body, fifteen
    steps from the fire, fifteen steps from the barsam and three steps from
    a righteous man." R.HF. p. 217.

passox 33, cont'd.

8. jāmag-i daštān kē xōnīh ud hixr paydāgīg pad-š.ud az-š
pad dastšōy pāk nē kunēd ud ō wārān abganēd.ēg-š wīnāh-i
hixr ō āb burdan ō bun.

9. ēn.pēš az wārān.gyāg-ē abganēd tā-š wāran pad-š be āyēd.
ān šāyēd.ka-š hixrōmandīh ēwāz az hamkarzagīh-i zan-i
daštān.ēg-iz. kas kē pad pēšag abāyēd šustan.uš hixrīh-i
paydāgīg pad-š nēst.ēd tōg abganēd.čiyōn čādur ud sarbar
ud wāšmag.

. If menstruation clothing which is visibly stained with blood and excrement, and which dastšōy washing would not [be sufficient to] clean , be exposed to rainfall then the sin of carrying excrement to water would afflict the soul [of the person who did it].

. As for the question regarding the necessary steps that should be taken when the menstruation clothing is left in open air prior to rainfall and later rain falls upon it. If the only defilement had been the result of direct contact with a menstruating woman, it should be washed by a professional person [of the rite of purification]. When this defilement is no longer visible it can be worn[1] like a veil or scarf or wāšmag [a type of head garment].

_____

pad tōg abganēd, lit. means lay down upon.

pursišn 34

1. mard-ē ēd kē rēman bawēd bē šōyēd.nō šabag ēk be dārēd.
    ān-i dudīgar tā dah roz nē kunēd.ka kunēd.har dō ke
    mānd ēstēd.pad ēk ēd rōz pādixšāihā kardan.ayāb az-š
    sē šabag mayān abāyēd kardan.agar zan bawēd.uš daštān
    rāy nō šabag be spōxtēd.dō pad ēk ēn pādixšā kardan ayā
    nē.

Because of the nature of this chapter, Dr. H.K. Mirza
of Bombay University kindly accepted to translate the
entire chapter.

Question 34

1. A man this, who is polluted, takes ablution.
    [Out of the period of] nine nights, he maintains
    [the rite] one [period of three nights]; that which
    is the sacred [period] up to the tenth day he does
    not practice. When he [so] practices, is it law-
    ful to observe each of the two [ablutions] which
    had remained, on one single day? Or should [a period
    of] three nights intervene [between two remaining
    ablutions]?

    If it is a woman, and on account of her menstruation,
    [a period of] nine nights has elapsed, [then] is it
    lawful to observe two [remaining ablutions] on one
    day?

passox 34

2. nō šabag dāštan sāmān ēn kū pas az šustan ī-š pad pēšag
sē rōz šabān tāh-ā-tāh[1]be pāyišn.ud ēk bār be šōyišn.

3. agar pad ham padisār.tā har sē šōyišn.hamē tāig az ān
hangām kunēd.ka-š nō šabag dāšt ud ka-š har sē pad ēn
ēwēnag šust tā ān be spōzīhēd.hamē ka be šōyēd.a-š az
ān hangām ka šōyēd. uš tāig tā ān-i did kunišn.uš sē rō
tāh-ā-tāh be pāyišn ud pas šōyišn.

4. dō pad ēk hangām nē pādixša šustan.ud agar-iz rōzgārān
was spōzīhēd.

5. ān-iz-i zanān hamgōnag.

6. ud ka nō rōz ayāb wēš pad dāstān nišast.hamē ka pad
gōmēz-i gāw ud āb šōyēd.ā-š nō šabag ēk-ē dāšt bawēd.

---

1. tāh-ā-tāh cf. Vd.5.2.,piece by piece, one by one, singly.

Answer 34

2. A limit of maintaining nine nights [is] this: after taking ablution, which is with ceremony, [a period of] three days and nights, one by one, should be maintained [between two ablutions]; and [then] ablution should be taken once.

3. If [it is] in the same beginning, up to each of the three ablutions, always it [the period] begins from that [beginning], when [a period of] nine nights is maintained; when he has taken ablution by each of the three [ablutions] in this manner, until that [period] elapsed, whenever one takes ablution [in this manner], then from that time when one takes ablution [in this manner], and its single [period of three nights] to the other [period] should be practiced, and its [period of] three days one by one should be maintained, and then one should take final ablution.

4. Two [ablutions] on one occasion is not lawful for ablution, and [it is so] even when more days [than three] have elapsed [between two ablutions].

5. Even the [case of] woman, [it is] in the same manner.

6. And if a woman remains in menstruation for nine days, or more, whenever she takes ablution with gōmēz of bull and water, then she shall have maintained one [out of] nine nights.

<u>passox 34</u>, cont'd.

7.   ud dō pad ēk hangām nē pādixšā šustan.čē hamē ka
        šoyēd.aš sē šabag-ē tāh-ā-tāh mayān abāyēd hištan.

Answer 34, cont'd.

7.   And two on one occasion is not lawful for ablution,

      because whenever one takes ablution, then [a period of]

      three nights, one by one, should be left between [two

      ablutions].

Note: In the Baršnūm Ceremony, after the initial ablution

      one has to undergo a retreat of nine nights. During

      that period of nine nights one has to take ablutions

      thrice at the intervals of three nights--that is after

      the third, sixth, and ninth night. The question is:

      if one undergoes Baršnūm retreat for only one period

      of three nights, is it lawful to take two more ablutions

      on one and the same occasion [that is, on the fourth

      day]?

pursišn 35

1. zan-ē kē frazand zāyēd.uš barūj[1] tā dō māh ayāb wēš

    az-š pāk nē bawēd.az ān-i hast ō wattar-rōn ne gardēd.

    ku-š gumānīgīh daštān abar oftēd.pad mehmānīh abar āb

    ud ātaš ud xwarišn ud dārišn ud pādyābīh pādixšā ka

    šawēd.ayāb čiyōn.

---

1. The reading as well as the transcription of this word is hypothetica
    I could not attest it in any of the accessible sources.

Question 35

1. A woman who has delivered a child, within two months or
    so her discharges do not become clean [do not stop] nor
    do they get worse, so much so that her suspicions fall
    on menstruation. Would it be permissible [under the
    circumstances] if while socializing (<u>pad mehmānīh</u>) she
    approaches water, fire, food, and provisions and
    [participates in the] ceremonial ablution? Or how
    [should it be?]

passox 35

2. hangirdīg ēn.kū zan-ē nōg zādag.tā čehel rōz.har ān
i az-š āyēd.bē agar ēwar paydāg kū daštān.tā pad ān
dārišn.pas az čehel rōz bē agar ēwar paydāg kū ān.tā
pad daštān dārišn.

3. hamē ka ēwar dānist kū nē az daštān.pad any[1] wimāmrīh
dārišn.pādixšā ka čiš-iz nē pahrēzēd.uš rāyīnišn čiyōn
pāk dārišn.

4. garāyīh daštān rāy saxttar nigerišn.ka hambun-iz
gumānīg pad-š bawēd.čiyōn ān i garīh[2] ō pahrēzišn.

---

1. Ank. reads hān

2. See translation, note 1 .

Answer 35

2. In brief, that is to say that: a post-partum woman (nōg zādag), for forty days should regard whatever exudes from her as lochia (ān) unless it is evident that it is menstruation. After forty days, unless it is clear that it is lochia, she should regard it as menstruation.

3. As soon as she realizes that it is not menstruation she should consider it as an illness, [in which case] it would be permissible if she does not follow the seclusion rules (pahrēzēd). Directions are as though she were clean.

4. Menstruation should be considered more serious than mange.[1] Even if she has doubt in her mind (bun), she should observe seclusion as it is observed in mange.

---

1. ـدلسؤ Ank. reads gerāyih-i. K.J. "Furthur to Ēmēt i Ašavahistān" Munchener Studien zur Spracwissenschaft, (Munchen, 1972), p. 67, reads the same and translates grievousness. So does Dr. Bishop of Columbia University. I think garīh means mange because even in modern Persian a similar contagious skin disease is called garī. Moreover, the same word occurs in ans. 37 which would be very far fetched if translated grievousness. For Persian gari compare Av. garenav, Bartholomae Dictionary Col. 515, Vd. 7-57. Yt. 13-131. Pahlavi transl. Vd. ۱۳ with explanation (āsnāg) signifying that the Pahlavi word has been well-known.

pursišn 36

1. mard-ē.ēd i akdēn čāh rōftan rāy.tan ō čāh barēd.ka
    abar āyēd.uš rēš-ē abar handām paydāg bawēd.
    dādestān-i ān čāh čē.agar nē dānēd kū ān rēš uš čē
    čiš pad-š bawēd.ayāb andar čāh.čiš-iz juttar bawēd
    ayāb nē.

passox 36

2. agar čiyōn abar nibišt.ēn-iz abāyēd nigerīdan kū rēš.
    ud xōn az-š āyēd.ayāb nē.

3. agar xōn az-š nē āyēd.ka-iz āyēd nasā nē šud ēstēd.
    pad im wināhkārīh ēd rēmanīh ēd čāh nēst.

4. ud agar nasā az-š šud ēstēd.pad im čāh ayāb bērōn
    gumānīg.kam wattar.

5. agar pad im čāh rēšēnidan[1] ēwar.nasā az-š šud ēstēd
    gumānīg.čāh pad nasā-pāk dārišn.az āb az-š wēxt ō
    pahrēzišn.tā ān kū sāl dranāy pad-š uzīhēd.

---

1. BTE. ⟨ᵚ⟩. Ank. reads rēsihastan, but mentions in TD
    ⟨ᵚ⟩. I think it is mis-script of ⟨ᵚ⟩.

1.   A [Zoroastrian] man   for the purpose of dredging
a well [belonging] to a Moslem, goes into the well.
on   coming out of the well he finds a visible
wound on his body. What is the prescription for that
well? If he is unaware of the cause of the wound,
whether it had happened inside the well, would it make
any difference or not?

Answer 36

2.   If, as written above, it should be investigated also,
whether the wound has been bleeding or not.

3.   If it did not bleed, or even if it did, and no defilement
exuded from it, [though in itself it is] a sin, the
well is not polluted.

4.   If defilement has exuded [but] it is uncertain whether
he has been wounded in the well or outside, the case
is less severe.

5.   If it is certain that he has been wounded in the well
and defilement has probably exuded, [then] the ceremony of nasā-pāk[1] for this well should be carried out.
Abstinence from the water coming out of that well should
be observed until a year is passed.

---

1.   Lit. corpse burning, [pāk from poxtan] here the ceremony of
nasā-pāk refers to the purification ceremony for the atonement
of this sin. Burning dead human matter is reckoned as the most
heinous of crimes in the Zoroastrian religion.

pursišn 37

1. pōst kē az dast ud abārīg handām bē šawēd.az-š ēč nam
    pad-š nē bawēd.hušk.rēš nē gīrēd.nasā bawēd ayāb nē.
    pad āb awiš burdan rēmanīh bawēd ayāb nē.agar hušk.rēš
    gīrēd. az ān ka nē gīrēd.čiš-iz juttar bawēd ayāb nē.

passox 37

2. pōst az dast pad ēn ēwēnag sawēd kū hušk.rēš-iz nē
    gīrēd.ēg-š nē nasā hast nē-iz garīh.

3. ud pad āb awiš burdan dādestān čiyōn pas ud pēš ud
    pēš az āb awiš barišnīh.pad dastšōy be kunišn.

4. ān i hušk.rēš gīrēd.pad hixrōmand-ē garīh dārišn.pad
    dastšōy šōyišn.tan rēmanīh ne bawēd.

Question 37

1. If the skin of hand or other limbs peels off, but
    without any moisture, [only] dry, [with] no wounding,
    should it be considered as a defilement or not? [If
    that affected limb] comes in contact with water, would
    it be pollution or not? If it is dry and without wound,
    would it be any different from the one which is with
    wound?

Answer 37

2. The skin of the hand which peels off dry as such that
    even does not cause a wound, is not a defilement, nor
    is it mange.

3. It is permissible to be exposed to water as long as before
    and after exposure to water, it undergoes dastšoy cleaning.

4. That dry [peeling] which causes wound, should be regarded
    as defilement of mange for which dastšoy washing suffices.
    There is no need for the tan rēman[1] procedure.

---

1. The Pahlavi word /ﻝ "rēman" Av. √ri = to ooze, to be foul, i.e.
    pus filth. So to purify oneself from pollution there are four stages
    of purification ceremony: pādyāb, nāhm, barešnūm, and rēman. See
    J. Modi, Religious Ceremonies and Customs of the Parsees. (Bombay,
    1922), pp. 87-154.

pursišn 38

1. kas kē ārd hamē srišēd.ka dast az ārd abar awurēd.
    ēg-š pōst az dast šud ēstēd.ēdōn kū-š andar handām nam
    abar nē paydāg bawēd.dādestān-i mard ud ārd čē.agar
    ān ārd be nān kunēd.pas pad ān gyāg kū-š pōst az-š
    šud ēstēd hušk.rēš nē gīrēd.dādestān be wardēd ayāb
    nē.

passox 38

2. pad-š nigerēd.pad ārd i srištag nasā pāyīh ēd nēst.ārd-i
    sriš az rēmanīh abēzār.

3. ud ārd-i asrīštag.bē agar im pōst pad-š paydāgīhēd.
    az srištag paydāgīhēd.ēg-š srištag hamāg pad hixrōmand
    dārišn.ō ātaxš nē barišn.ud pad xwarišn sag ud vāy šāyēd
    pad ān-i mardomān hixrōmandīh rāy.nē šāyēd.

Question 38

1.   He who kneads flour, while taking his hand off the
flour [some] pustules of his hand fall off in such a
way that no wetness is visible on the limb. What is
the religious view regarding this man as well as the
flour? If he makes that flour into bread and later
that spot of the hand which had peeled off does not
develop any wound, would this alter the judgement or
not?

Answer 38

2.   Bear in mind that there is no [need for] defilement
precaution regarding kneaded flour. The kneaded flour
is free from defilement.

3.   As for unkneaded flour, if this peeled skin is visible
in it, then the whole flour should be regarded defiled.
[Therefore] should not be taken to the fire (baking
oven). It should be utilized for dog and bird food.
On the account of [its] defilement it would not be
suitable for men's [consumption].

passox 38, cont'd.

4.   ka.nān kardan rāy.be ō ātaxš barēd.wīnāh-iz hixr ō
ātaxš burdan bawēd.ka-iz nān be kard.ēg-iz az
hixrōmandīh nē abēzār ud pad xwarišn-i wehān nē šāyēd.

5.   hušk.rēš pad-š bawišnīh rāy.dādestān im abar nibišt

Answer 38, cont'd

4.   Since, for making bread, it [the kneaded flour] should

be taken to the fire [baking oven], the sin of taking

defilement to the fire would also apply to that. Even

that baked bread would not be free from defilement and

would not be suitable for the consumption of the Zoro-

astrians.[1]

5.   As for the dry wound, the judgement is the same as

mentioned above.

---

1.   Wehān, lit. means the good ones. Since Weh-dēn is another term
designating adherents of the Zoroastrian faith, then Wehān might
be an abbreviation of Weh-denān, coined by the scribe.

pursišn 39

1. ēn.ku.mardōm.ka widarān bawēnd.uš-ān tā rōz-i ristāxēz.
    dādestān čiyōn bawēd.

2. ka-šān.pad ōš-i sēdīgar. āmār kunēnd.az kirbag.kē-šān
    az widarišnīh frāz kunēnd.sūd čē bawēd.

3. petītīgīh pad gōwišn.ka kunēnd rāh ō dušox bandēd ayāb
    nē.

Question 39

1. [The question is] this. When people pass away, what happens to them until the day of resurrection?

2. Since on the third dawn [after death] they will be [religiously] evaluated, what would be the benefit [for their souls] of meritorious deeds performed for them after their death.

3. The verbal repentance[1] which people exercise, does it close the path to hell or not?

---

1. Verbal repentance "petīt" is of great significance in Zoroastrian religion, the performance of which for the redemption of soul, is a daily obligation. "If a person cannot recite the petīt daily, then he should order another person to perform petīt for him. There is no difference between these two recitals, that is when recited by another person the effect would be such as if performed by him himself. If it is not performed during lifetime, it should be performed during the three nights after one's death. The dignity of each session of the recitation of petīt lasts for three days, that is if one dies within those three days it is the same as if he had recited petīt at the time of his death." R.HF., pp. 32-3.

"The performance of petīt has only a religious effect. It saves the sinner from penalties in the other world, but not from those here below. It delivers him before God but not before man." Introd. Vd. V. P.C.. SBE. vol. 4.tr. Darmesteter. Also op. cit. 3. sec. 20, and 9. sec. 49-50.

The shortest petīt formulae that should be recited daily is: "I am sorrowing for, and repentant and in renunciation of every sin which I have spoken, which I have done, which has arisen through me and which I have ignored". R.HF., p. 32.

For lengthy details see, J.P. Asmussen, X̌wāstvānift, (Acta Theologica Danica, Copenhagen, 1965), pp. 40-90.

pursišn 39, cont'd.

4. ud agar bandēd ēg-šān gāh kū gyāg bawēd.

5. ruwān-i wināhkārān.kē be ō dušox šawēd pēš az tan-i pasēn. az dušox rastār bawēnd ayāb nē.

6. ka-šān petītīg nē kard.uš wināh nē puhlēnēd.ēg-š andar dušox kār čiyōn bawēd.

7. ruwān-i šudagān andar dušox kē pāyēd.

8. kē-š kirbag wināh rāst.ān kē-š kam ud wēš bawēd. dādestān čē.

9. ruwān-i widardagān.pēš az tan-i pasēn.ēk ōy-i did wēnēnd. u-šān mihr dōšāram ud āšnāgīh bawēd ayāb nē.

10. hangird.andar ēn dar pursišn čand ast.wizīr ēk ēk wizīdartar šāyēd šnaxtan·ud ka ēk-iz ēk paydāg niwisīhēnd pad nō brīn kardan.har ēk.čiyōn az weh dēn paydāg. passox abar azabarnibišt.

Question 39, cont'd.

4. And if it does close, then where would their station be?

5. Will the souls of the sinful ones who go to hell be liberated from hell before the tan-i pasēn[1] or not?

6. What would be the condition in hell of those who have not repented and their sins have not been atoned?

7. Who protects the soul of the departed in hell?

8. What would be the prescription for him whose benefactions and sins balance, as well as him whose [benefactions and sins] is either less or more [does not balance]?

9. Would the souls of the departed [ones] meet one another before tan-i pasēn? Would they feel love, affection and recognition or not?

10. In short, there are several questions in this chapter. The judgement concerning each one of them is clearly recorded, it [the whole composition] will be divided into nine sections, each of which will have the answer in accordance with the religious law pertinent to the above written [questions] (passox abar azabar nibišt) [i.e. under each question will be its answer].

---

1. The ultimate form of existence the universe will be given after the current cycle has elapsed. H.S. Nyberg, A Manual of Pahlavi, (Otto Harrassowitz, Wiesbaden, 1974), II, 190.

247

ān i fradom[1]

11. ēn.ku.mardōm ka widarišn bawēnd ēg-šān tā rōz ristāxiz

dādestān čiyōn bawēd wizirīdan framāyēd.pad yazdān kām

---

1. In MS. TD2 there are no separate divisions as Ank. has arranged
in BTE. The sections are in continuous lines. Only the words
passox[s] are written with red ink and as from section sašom the
nominal numbers are written in red ink too.

Question 39, cont'd.

The First Question

11.   [The question is] this: when people die what happens

to them until the day of resurrection?   Please explain

[it], by the grace of deities.[1]

---

[1] pad yazdān kām literary means 'in compliance with the wishes of the deities'.

249

12. dādestān-šān ēdōn bawēd kū tan-šān abar zamīg.ast-ē
     ō āb.ud ast-ē o urwar.ast-ē ō vād gumēzēd.

13. ruwān ō mēnōgān āmār i pad stōš ō činwadpuhl rasēd.
     ka-š āmār-i pad stōš pad-š bawēd.agar ahlaw.abar frāx
     činwadpuhl.urwāhmīhā widarēd.ud ast ō garodmān.ast ō
     wahišt.ast ō hammistagān franawēd.agar druwand.az mayān
     tēz bārīg puhl frahist bīmīhā ō ērang dušox oftēd.

dudigar

14. ēn.kū ka-šān.pad ōšbām-i sēdīgar.āmār kunēnd.az kirbag
     kē-šān az widarišnīh frāz kunēnd.sūd čē bawēd.

passox 39

12. Their state would be thus: their body [will remain]
on the earth, part[1] of it will mingle with water, part
of it with plants, and   part with air.

13. The soul will depart for celestial judgement which
takes place at činwad[2] bridge on the fourth day after
death, when the celestial judgement of the fourth day
after death takes place.   If the soul is righteous, it
will   joyfully   pass through the wide činwad bridge,
and will go either to garodmān, "highest section of
the Heavens", or to   paradise or to the hammistagan,
"the neutral station between heaven and hell."   If it
is sinful,   it will fall into the wretched hell   from
the middle of the sharp narrow bridge, with a great
deal of fear.

The Second

14. This: since the [celestial] reckoning will be held on
the third dawn after death, what benefit would the departed gain from the meritorious deeds performed for him?

---

1.   ast-ē, K.J. translates "either", "Ēmēt-i Ašavahištan", Kuruš Mem.
Vol. (Bombay, 1974)

2.   The divider bridge which separates the souls of the righteous
dead who cross from those of the wicked who fall off.

passox 39, cont'd.

passox

15. sūd-šān wuzurg ōwōn bawēd kū-šān pad sazāgīhā paywand.
kū.kirbag.kē-šān frāz az widarišnīh kunēnd.andāzag ud
paymānag čand ān čand sālān i was.tā-iz madan-i sošyans
kunīhēd.hamāg andar āmār-i stōš ōh āmār girēnd.ud ast
i-š pādifrāh kāhēnēd.ud· ast i-š az wināh i kard
hangārihēd.ast i-š urwāhm mehgāh-i ruwān abzāyēd bawēd.
ka-š ruwān pad-š bōzihēd.ō ān-i pahlom axwān rasēd.

16. az im čim.kirbag-i.pas az be widarišnīh-i kas kardan
rāy.frayād ast-ē ō ruwān-i widardagān.mayān ān-i mard
andar zīwēndagīh xwad kunēd ayāb ō kas framāyēd.tā ān
i pas az be widarišnīh.ēn hast kū ān-i andar zīwēndagīl
hamē kunīhēd.a-š hamē rawēd.nōg nōg ēk abar did.hamē
abzāyēd.ud ān i pas az be widarišnih ān and bawēd čand
kunīhēd.ā-š ēdōn nē rawēd.

Answer 39, cont'd.

Answer

45. Their benefit would be great in this way, that through
this expedient link, the meritorious deeds which are
practiced [by the survivors] after the passing away
[of a person], will be reckoned [on the departed] on
the judgement day of stōs̆, in all the quantity and proportion in as many years they [good deeds] are
performed even to the final days of the advent of
Sos̆yāns.[1] It decreases his retribution; [it helps]
his sins to be considered [favorably]; it [helps to]
increase the delight and grandeur of the soul.
When his soul is [thus] redeemed it will reach the
foremost existence.

46. For this reason a benefaction which is practiced after
the death of a person will be of help to the soul of
the departed. [The difference] between those [benefac-
tions] that a man practices himself during his lifetime
and those that he instructs others to perform [for him]
after his death is this, that the ones which are performed in lifetime will go to him one by one, each
will be added to the other. [But] that which is done
after his passing away, as many as they might be, would
not reach him in the same manner.

---

1. Savior, especially the final savior who will bring about the
Fras̆agird, the ultimate Renovation.

passox 39, cont'd.

sēdīgar

17.   ēn kū.pētitīgīh.i pad gōwiš̌n ka gōwēnd.rāh ō dušox
      bandēd ayāb nē.

18.   agar bandēd.ēg-š̌ān gāh kū gyāg bawēd.

19.   passōx ēn dō andar ēk.

20.   pētitīgīh-i pad gōwiš̌n gōwēnd.ka meniš̌nīgīhā.abartar
      ān i pēš̌ abēzag rāst andar dastwarān andar dēnāgāhān.
      tōziš̌n-i wināh ud čandīh kirbag š̌nāsān ^{1} gōwīhēd.ud ān
      i-š̌ ēd abēzagān gōwēnd niyōxš̌ēd kār uš̌ kunēd.azēr saxt
      bandēd rāh-i dušox.

21.   agar kas-ē pad ān ēwēnag nē mad ēstēd.pēš̌-i wehān mad
      ēstēd.meniš̌nīgīhā ud ruwān dōstīhā wināh dušmenīh gōwē
      hamgōnag pad bandiš̌n-i ān dušwidarag rāh meh frayād.^{2}

_____

1.   Ank. reads š̌nāsān. See plate.

2.   Ank. reads frahixt, so does K.J., "Ēmēt-i Ašavahīstān", Kuruš̌ Mer
      Vol., (Bombay, 1974), p. 168.

Answer 39, cont'd.

The Third

17. Would verbal repentance, when uttered, close the path
to hell or not?

18. If it closes, then where will their [the repenters']
station be?

19. The answer to these two questions is one and the same.

20. Verbal repentance when uttered thoughtfully, particularly that which is [performed] before holy and
righteous priests and religious authorities who know
about the types of the sins and their atonements, ·
[provided one] listens to and practices [verbally]
the repentance of sin which would be uttered by these
holy ones,   will firmly close the path to hell
underneath. [i.e. if one repeats thoughtfully and accu-
rately the repentance formulae uttered by the priest,
it will keep him away from hell.]

21. If a person with such qualifications [being a holy religious authority] is not available, one should utter
whole-heartedly his aversion towards sin and his love
for the soul before believers of the Zoroastrian religion. In this way, a great help [is provided] for the
closing of that evil path.

passox 39, cont'd.

22.   ud ka-š gōwišnīg rāh bast.pad ān-i abardom.ayāb ān-i

nidom.pāyag-i az kirbag wināh čiyōn-š handōxt ēstēd uš

hast.ēg-š pad stōš āmār pad-š bawēd.uš gāh-ē ruwān.kirḇ

pad sazāgīhā.ast i hammistagān.ast i wahištīg.ast i

grōdmānīg.

čahārom

23.   ēn·kū ruwān-i wināhkārān kē be ō dušox šawēd.pēš az tan‹

pasēn.az dušox rāstār šāyēd bawēd ayāb nē.

passox

24.   ruwān-i druwandān wēš wināhān.ka ō dušox ōbast hēnd.tā

tan-i pasēn uš rāstār nē bawēnd.

panjom

25.   ēn.kū.ka-š pētītīgīh nē kard.uš wināh nē purr.a-š anda‹

dušox kār čiyōn.

Answer 39, cont'd.

22.   When the path becomes closed by these words, whether at
       the uppermost or the lowermost, the place of his soul
       according to the accumulation of his benefactions and
       sins at the reckoning of the third dawn would be either
       in the neutral station between heaven and hell or in
       paradise or in the highest station in Heavens.

The Fourth

23.   The souls of the sinful ones which go to hell; would they
       be liberated before the time of tan-i pasēn or not?

Answer

24.   The souls of the unrighteous, great sinners which have
       fallen into hell will not be liberated until the time of
       the tan-i pasēn.

The Fifth

25.   A person who did not repent, [yet] his sin is not
       [viewed as] full-fledged, what would be his position in
       hell?

passox 39, cont'd

passox

26. har ān kē ō dušox ōbast.ēg-š andar dušox pādifrāh pad
ān andāzag bawēd ke-š wināh kard ēstēd.ka-š pad ān
andāzag abar mad.ēg-š andar dušox ēwāz pīm-i az gyāg
bawēd.pādifrāh nē.

šašom

27. ēn.kū.ruwān-i šudagān andar dušox kē pāyēd.

passox

28. ruwān-i šudagān i mēnōg-i dādestān pāyēd.dādār abar-š
xwēš dāmān wistardag.uš amāwandīh ud ōzōmandīh har
gyāg rasišnīg.az ān-i azērīgdom dušox tā ān-i abardom
garōdmān.ōwōn ōzōmand ud amāwand i-š.az hamāg gyāg.har
kas must ud adādīh abāz dāštan ud spōxtan tuwān.

Answer

26. Anyone who has fallen into hell, his retributions in hell
would proportionately equal his sin. When this is ba-
lanced, there remains only the discomfort of being in -
side hell; there is no [other] punishment.

The Sixth

27. Who will protect the souls of the departed ones in hell?

Answer

28. The soul of the departed is protected by the Spirit of
Justice whom the Creator spread throughout His Creations.
He reaches everywhere with power and vigour, from the
lowermost hell to the uppermost garōdmān.[1] So powerful
and vigorous is he that he is able to withhold and reject
distress and injustice from anyone.

---

1. The highest celestial abode.

passox 39, cont'd.

29. ēn-iz.kū.ruwān-i widardagān druwandān ham ruwān-i mardē
kē dādār-i weh āfrīd ēstēd.ušān bun gōhr weh ud
yazdānīg pad-š.ud wahištagīh-i az rāh-i yazdān ud
aburdframānīh ud wadkunišnīh-i xwēš rāy. ā-šān ruwān ē
dušox mad estēd.ušān az nēmag-i yazdān ēd ōzōmandīh
pad-š be mānēd kū dēwān.andar dušōx frāy az wināh i-šā
kard ēstēd.pādifrāh pad-š ā-šān kardan nē tuwān.ud dēw
rāy xwad ān nērōgōmandīh nēst.i-šān dādestān juttarīnī
kam ud wēš pad-š kardan.nē tuwān.

30. ēn-iz.kū hamāg ruwānān.hangirdīgīha nērog-i az ummēd
ristāxēz ud tan-i pasēn.āmurzišn-ē az yazdān abdom pad
šān hast.dēwān ān-iz i xwad abesīhišn ud apaydāgīh i-š
abdom pad-š bawēd.mālēnd.uš-ān ān rāy nērōg kāstag.

Answer 39, con't.

29. This too [should be pointed out]: the souls of the sinful
ones are also the souls [of humans] which the Good
Creator has created. In essence it is good, divine, and
heavenly. Because of their deviation from the path of
the deities and their disobedience and evil-doing, their
souls have entered hell. In the realm of the deities
this power remains for them: the demons who are in hell
cannot punish them beyond what their sins have been.
Because the demons themselves are not sufficiently
powerful to alter justice. They are not capable of
adding to or diminishing it.

30. This too [should be mentioned]: all souls have a hope
for ristāxēz[1] and tan-i pasēn and for the ultimate
forgiveness of the deities. The demons also because of
the prospect of their ultimate destruction and disappear-
ance[2] attack [each other] and because of that [continual
conflict] their strength diminishes.

---

1. Resurrection of the dead.

2. In Bd. Chapter 28, on the evil doing of Ahrēman and the demons,
the same conception is expressed: the devil army is doomed to
annihilation because of the creation of the demon Āz "greediness,"
because he devours everything and when through destitution nothing
remains he eats himself. SBE. V, p. 110, tr. West.

261

31. ēn-iz.kū.dušox andar zamīg hast-i ohrmazd dād.ud agar-i
ōh kū.pad meh dādestānīh gyāg-i ganāgmēnōg ud dēwān būd
ēstēd.ēg-iz uš ān nērōgmandīh hast kū-š dēwān az pādifr
i nē abāyēd kardan abāz dāštan tuwān.ud ān rāy.ka-šān.
pad tan-i pasēn. rastār bawēd.az nigerišn ān abartarān
wuzurg zōhrān yazdān nē brahnag hēnd.

32. ud ruwān-i dušoxīgān andar dušōx ēg-šān pānāg ud pādār
pad ān ēwēnag hast-i čiyōn abar nibišt paydāgēnēd.

haftom

33. ēn-iz.kū.kē-š kirbag wināh rāst.ān kē-š kam ud wēš bawē
dādestān čē.

passox

34. kē-š kirbag wināh rāst.ēg-š dādestān ēn kū hammistagān.
kē-š kirbag wēš kū wināh.ā-š ruwān pad ān-i pāhlom axwā
pāyag passazagīhā.kē wināh wēš az kirbag dušoxīg.

Answer 39, cont'd.

31. This too: [should be mentioned] **hell** is within
the earth which is created by Ohrmazd. And even if,
[it] so happens, through great judiciousness, that the
place of the demons be there [earth] yet He is so powerful that He is able to prevent the demons from imposing
undue punishment. Therefore when they [those who are
punished] are redeemed on the day of tan-i pasēn [it
signifies that] they have not been devoid of the [minute]
surveillance of the supreme, powerful deities.

32. [So] the souls of the hellish people in hell have their
own protector and guardian as [already] mentioned and
illustrated above.

The Seventh

33. This also: what is the judgement regarding him whose
benefactions balance his sins and him whose [benefac-
tions and sins] are either less or more [do not balance]?

Answer

34. The judgement for him whose benefactions and sins balance
is that his place would be in hammistagān [i.e. the neutral
place between hell and heaven]. He whose benefactions are
more than his sins, the stage of his soul['s abode] fit-
tingly is [in] the best existence [i.e. paradise]. He whose
sins are more than his benefactions [the stage of his soul
would be] hellish.

passox <u>39</u>, cont'd.

haštom

35. ēn.kū.ruwān-i widardagān.pēš az tan-i pasēn.ēk ōy i did
wēnēnd.uš-ān mihr dōšāram ud āšnāgīh bawēd ayāb nē.

passox

36. ēn.kū.ruwān-i ahlawān.i ēk ōy did wēnēnd.hamayār hēnd.
uš-ān mehr ud dōšāram ēk abāz ōy-i did bowandagīhā.

37. ān-i druwandān ēk ōy-i did nē wēnēnd har ēk andar dušox
ōwōn menēnd čiyōn pad tan   ēd hē.ud kas pad jud az ōy p
dušox nēst.

38. abar dušoxīgān garāntom čiš ēd ēwtāgīh hast.

The Eighth

5.   This: will the souls of the departed meet one
      another before the tan-i pasēn?   Will they feel love,
      compassion, and recognition or not?

Answer

6.   The souls of the righteous ones see each other; they
      help each other. Their love and affection for one
      another will be perfect.

7.   Those [souls] of the sinners will not meet each other.
      Each one [of them] in hell thinks himself to be alone,
      that there is no one but him in the hell.

8.   To those in hell, the most grievous thing is this loneli-
      ness.

pursišn 40

1. čiš-i gētig pad brēh ayāb pad kunišn.

2. kirbag warzīdārīh ud wināh kunišnīh kē mardomān kunēnd
   az baȷ̌ōbaxt ayāb az hāzišn yazdān ud tomīgān.

3. kē-š xwāstag-ē ayāb any nēkīh baxt ēstēd.uš pad-š
   nē tuxšēd.ā-š awiš rasēd ayāb nē.

4. baxt ud spihr har dō ēk. ušān nērōg az rošnān ayāb az
   tomīgān.ud agar az rošnān.čē rāy petyāragīh baxšēnd.
   ud agar az tomīgān.nēkīh čiyōn baxšēnd.

5. ud zamān ud brīn ud astānag pad panāhīh šāyēd spōxt
   ayāb nē.

6. Wināh ud kirbag warzīdan abāg kunišn ud brēhīnišn ayār
   ayāb nē.

Question 40

1. Are worldly affairs [governed] by destiny or by deeds?

2. Are the good deeds and sins which people do motivated by Providence or by the incitement of deities and the inhabitants of the world of darkness?[1]

3. He to whom wealth or other privileges are allotted, [if] he does not make efforts for [obtaining] it, would it go to him or not?

4. Are destiny and the Celestial Governing Sphere the same? Does their power originate from [the world of] the luminaries [i.e. supreme God Ohrmazd], or from [the world of] darkness [i.e. Ahreman]? If from the luminaries, why do they allot adversity? If from darkness, how is it that they allot favors?

5. Would it be possible to avert time, destiny and misfortune through protection?

6. Is the practice of sin or benefaction associated with deeds and destiny, or not?

---

1. tamigān; the world of darkness implies demonic power. In the Zoroastrian concept as reflected in Bd. 1, Ohrmazd [the supreme God] is the infinite luminary [force] against Evil [force] which is infinite darkness and prevails over the world of darkness.

passox 40

7. ēn šaš brīn hast.ka passox-i ān ēk ēk judāg bawēd
    paydāgtar.

fradom

8. ēn.kū.čiš-i gētig pad brēh ayāb pad kunišn.

passox

9. ast-ē pad brēh.ud ast{ē] pad kunišn.ast{ē] pad nērōg
    har dō pad-š paydāgīhēd.

dudīgar

10. ēn.kū.kirbag warzīdārīh wināh warzidārīh kē mardom
    kunēnd.az baǰōbaxt ayāb az hāzišn-i yazdān ud tamigān.

passox

11. kirbag warzīdārīh ud wināh warzīdārīh kē mardom kunēnd
    az kardārīh-i ān mardōm kē kunēnd.ušān.ēd rāy.pad
    kirbag pādišn ud pad wināh pazd abar bawēd.ud agar az
    baǰōbaxt hē.ēg-šān pad kirbag mizd xwēšīh.ud pad wināh
    pazd.abar kunišnīh nē dādestānīg hē.

Answer 40

7.   This [question] comprises six sections. If the answer to each one is given separately, it will be more clear.

First

8.   This: whether worldly affairs are (governed) by destiny or will power?

Answer

9.   A part is by destiny and a part is by free will and a part seems [to be governed] through the force of both.

Second

10.   This: is the act of sin and benefaction practised by people motivated by Providence or by the incitement of the deities and the inhabitants of the world of darkness?

Answer

11.   The act of benefaction or sin which people perform is [entirely] the performance of those who do it. For this reason there is reward for their benefaction and retribution for their sin. Had it been allotted by Providence, then execution of reward for benefaction and retribution for sin upon their action [which had been beyond their control] would have been unjust. [Injustice is not the quality of Providence.]

passox 40, cont'd.

12.   az wehdēn ēn-iz paydāg.kū yazdān ud dēwān mēnōgīhā ō

meniš̆n-i mardōm ōh rasēnd.uš̆ān yazdān ō kirbag.

warzīdārīh ud dēwān ō wināh kardan ō hāzēnd.

sēdīgar

13.   ēn.kū.kē-š̆ xwāstag ayāb nēkīh-ē baxt ēstēd.uš̆ pad-š̆

nē toxš̆ēd.aš̆ awiš̆ rasēd ayāb nē.

passox

14.   az weh dēn paydāg.ku. ān i baxt ēstēd.hast frārōn

tuxš̆āgīh rāy zūdtar rasēd.hast wināhkārīh rāy az-š̆

appār bēd.

čahārom

15.   ēn.ku.baxt spihr har dō ēk.uš̆-ān nērōg az rōš̆nān ayāb

az tomigān.agar az rōš̆nān.čē rāy petyāragīh baxš̆ēnd.aga

az tomigān.čim nēkīh baxš̆ēnd.

Answer 40, cont'd.

12.   This also is revealed in the Zoroastrian religion that
      [both] deities and demons intangibly penetrate the
      minds of people so that deities encourage benefactions
      and the demons encourage sin.

The Third

13.   This: he to whom wealth or other favors are allotted,
      [if] he does make efforts for [obtaining] it, would it
      go to him or not?

Answer

14.   It is revealed in the Zoroastrian religion that that
      which is allotted may reach [the person] more quickly
      on account of [his] righteous aims, and might be taken
      away from him on account of his sins.

The Fourth

15.   This: are destiny and the Celestial Governing Sphere
      the same? Is their power through the luminaries or
      the world of darkness? If from the luminaries, why
      do they distribute adversity, and if from the world
      of darkness how is it that they allot favors?

Answer 40, cont'd.

16. ēn saxwan šebišnīg.čē.ast-ē pursišnīg.ast-ē wizīrīg.

hangirdīg passox.ēn.kū.baxt spihr har dō nē ēk.čē.

baxt ān i brēhēnišnīg.ud spihr ān i kunišnīg.az-iz

ēn paydāg kū dō hast.uš-ān jud jud nērōg az rōšnān

az tomigān bawēd.ān i az rōšnān bawēd petyārag nē

baxšēd.ud ān i az tomigān bawēd nēkīh nē baxšēd.

panjom

17. ēn.ku.zamān ud brīn ud astānag pad panāhīh šāyēd
spōxtan ayāb nē.

passox

18. ēn.kū.zamān ud brīn bē pad dādār nērōg any spōxtan nē
šāyēd.

19. pad hast hangām kē-š mēh sūdīh-i weh dām rāy.hast ka-š
brīn zamān spoxtan.az weh dēn paydāg.ēn ēwāzīgīhā.nē
amargānīgīhā.

Answer 40, cont'd.

Answer

16. This is a confusing statement because it is partly
     a question and partly an answer. A brief answer is
     that destiny and the Celestial Governing Sphere are
     not the same. Because destiny (baxt) is fated and
     the Celestial Governing Sphere relates to free will.
     Therefore, it is evident that they are two indivi-
     dual forces each of which are from [arise from] the
     luminaries and from the world of darkness. That
     which is [derived] from the luminaries will not
     distribute adversity and that which is from the world
     of darkness will not allot favors.

The Fifth

17. This point: could time, destiny and misfortune
     be possibly averted through protection?

Answer

18. This: time and destiny cannot be averted other than by
     the force of the Creator.

19. As revealed in the Zoroastrian religion, there are
     times when for the better benefit of the good creatures
     He has to avert time and destiny. This is exceptional,
     not general.

passox 40, cont'd.

20. astānag pad ayārīh ud pānagīh abarag[1] yazdān i spōzīhēd
    ud nē rasēd.

šašom

21. ēn.kū.kirbag ud wināh warzīdan abāg kunišn ud
    brēhēnišn ayār ayāb nē.

passox

22. hangirdīg.kū.wināh ud kirbag har dō pad kunišn bawēd.
    ud brēhēnišnīg čiš az yazdān az-iz dēwān bawēd.

23. ud yazdān ō kirbakkārān ud kirbakkārān ō yazdan
    ayār hēnd.bazakkārān ō dēwān.dēwan pad-iz bazakkārān
    anāgīh kardār.a-šān ōh pazd ud pādifrāh rasēnīdār hēnd.

---

1.   𐭠𐭯𐭥𐭩 Ank. reads abārig, so does K.J. in "Ēemēt i Ašavahišta:
   Kuruš Mem. Vol., (Bombay, 1974), p. 174 and translates accordingly
   also M.F. Kanga in his rendering of the same question (pub. Bombay
   1975) reads the same. I believe it must be a mis-script of 𐭠𐭫𐭢
   or   𐭠𐭯𐭥 , otherwise the translation would be confusing.

Answer 40, cont'd.

20. Misfortune can be stopped and averted through the help
and protection of the lofty deities.

The Sixth

21. This: whether the practice of benefaction or sin is
associated with will power and destiny?

Answer

22. In short, sin and benefaction are both related to will
power. The affair of destiny relates to deities and
demons both.

23. The deities are associates of the righteous and vice
versa. The demons associate with the evil-doer sinners
and vice versa. Thus, they [the demons] are the con-
veyor of retribution and punishment to them [the sinners].

pursišn 41

1. wināhīhā-i nāmčist.čiyōn daštānmarz ud kūnmarz ud
   jehmarz.abārīg wināhīhā.i har ēn zamān nibišt.wizārišn
   tōzišn gētīg framāyēd nibištan.

2. kadār kirbag kē ēn wināhīhā be rōbēd.wizārišn šnāyišnīh[1]
   bawēd.

---

1. ᘱᕟᖟᖕᕟᘱ both Ank. and K.J. "Ēmēt i Ašvahištan", Kuruš Mem. Vol.,
   (Bombay, 1974), p. 176, read šōyišnih and translate "purification".
   I think it is mis-script ᘱᕟᖟᕽᕽᖕᘱ which would make more sense.

Question 41

1. Would you please explain worldly atonement for certain sins such as copulation during menstruation, sodomy, prostitution and other sins which are recorded[1] so far [har ēn zamān], so that it may be written down.

2. Which benefaction would remove these sins? [Your] comments would be [much] appreciated.

---

1. Refers to the list of sins and atonements enumerated in matigān and dadistān and rivāyāts.

passox 41

3. kūnmarz wināhīhā margarzānīh.uš gētīgīha tozišn ōzadan.

4. daštānmarz wināh ēd i abēr garāy.bē nē margarzān.uš
   tōzišnīh andar weh dēn paydāg ēstēd.uš gōkān and drang.

5. jehmarz was ēwēnag hast grāntar.

6. ān-i kam wināhtar ān ka-š.andar ham daštān māh.marzišn
   i az any mard pad-š nē būd ēstēd.ud im jeh nē ābus az
   any mard.uš šōy nēst.ka-š.az ēn sē ēk-iz pad-š nēst.ka
   marzēd.marzīdār šast stīr wināh.

7. čē.agar-š.andar ham daštān māh. any mard marzēd az ān
   marzišn.marzīdār kamest tanāpuhl ēd wināh.

8. agar-š ābusīh bawēd.uš any mard marzēd.az ān marzišn
   ābusīh tabāhēd.marzīdār margarzān.

9. agar zamānīg ābusīh nē tabāhēd.bē-š wizend abar rasēd.
   ēg-š dō tanāpuhl wināh.

Answer 41

3.   The sin of sodomy deserves death. The worldly
     atonement for it would be killing [the sinner].

4.   The sin of copulation during menstruation is grievous,
     but does not deserve death. Atonement for it has been
     explained in the Zoroastrian religion in lengthy detail.

5.   Prostitution has many types. Some are more grievous
     than others.

6.   The one which is less sinful is this: if during men-
     struation no intercourse has taken place with another
     man, nor has this prostitute become pregnant from
     another man, nor has she a husband. If none of these
     three [conditions] holds and she copulates, the sin
     of the copulator is sixty stīr.

7.   Because if she had copulated with another man during
     her menstruation, on this [recent] copulation, the
     least sin for the copulator would be tanāpuhl.

8.   If she is pregnant, yet she copulates with another
     man and owing to that copulation abortion happens, the
     copulator deserves death.

9.   If for a while abortion does not happen but injury is
     caused, then two tanāpuhl sins [would be accounted
     against the copulator].

passox 41, cont'd.

10. ud agar frazand zāyēd.uš.ān marzišn rāy apādyāwandīh
    kamīh abar tan-i im zāyišn mad ēstēd.agar.az ān mēh
    apādyāwandīh.tā čehel rōz pad-š wardēd.mīrēd.marzīdār
    margarzān bawēd.andar im zāyišn hamēmālomand.

11. ud agar im jeh šōy hast.marzīdār andar šōy jeh pad sī
    sad stīr tozišnōmand.

12. abārīg wināhihā pad ham hangōšīdag gōkān and drang.ka
    pursēd.tozišn čiyōn az dēn paydāg.niwēsēm.

Answer 41, cont'd.

10. If she delivers a child, and owing to that copulation
     weakness and deficiency appear in this offspring, and
     if forty days pass and from that major ailment [the
     offspring] dies, the copulator deserves death [and]
     will be accused of [the death of] this offspring.

11. If this prostitute has a husband, the copulator
     should recompense three hundred st̄irs to that husband.

12. I will also point out [niwēsem] in detail and length
             other sins and the nature of their atonements,
     when you inquire.

pursišn 42

1. kē-š wināh-ē abag zan-ē akdēn gādan jahēd.ud az ān
   gādan frazand andar aškamb frāz bawēd.ēg-š wināh čē.ud
   agar nē bawēd wināh čand.ud agar ān zan šōyindag.ud ān
   frazand ō frazām rasēd.uš pad akdēnīh parwarēnd.ud agar
   ān frazand andar aškamb ayāb bērōn ōzenēnd.agar ān zan
   dōšīzag.ud agar ān zan weh dēn.eg-šān dādestān ēk ēk čē

Question 42

He who commits the sin of consortium with a Moslem woman and due to that consortium a child is conceived in
the womb, then what is the [degree of that] sin? If
there is not [any conception] then what would be the
[the degree of that] sin? If she gets married and that
child is born and is brought up as a Moslem [what would
be the degree of the sin], and if that child is killed
either in the womb or outside [what would be the degree
of the sin] or if that woman had been a virgin, or if
she had been a Zoroastrian, what would be the prescription
for each case?

passox 42

2. agar-š čiš andar nēst.i ān rāy juttar.weh dēn mard kē
    zan-i akdēn gāyēd.az im gādan ābust ān bawēd.ēg-š fraza:
    ō akdēn dādan rāy.zamānīg tanāpuhl wināh.

3. ud agar frazand zāyēd.ayāb andar ēškamb-i im zan mīrēd
    ud nasā kunēd.har wināh.i andar akdēnīh pad-š kunīhēd.
    ō bun.ud andar ēn was ēwēnag wināh-i čand-iz marzišn
    šāyēd būd.

4. ud agar frazand be ō pānzdah sālag rasēd.ud pad akdēnīh
    ēstēd.i-š.pad akdēnīh ēstādan rāy.gādār margarzān.

5. ud agar ziyānag šōyīnīg.andar šōy pad-iz gādan tāwān
    tōzīšnōmand.ud gādan nō sad stīr bawēd pad hamēmālān ^{1}
    wināh.

6. zan dōšīzag dōšīzagīh burdan rāy.tanāpuhl ēd wināh.

7. ud agar weh dēn hast gādan rāy tāwān ō šōy ayāb sālār-i
    ziyānag kunišn.tōzišn dōšīzagīh ham andar šōy ayāb sālār
    i ziyānag kunišn.

---

1. There are three kinds of sins: <u>wināh-i ruwānīg</u>, <u>wināh-i
    hamēmālān</u>, and <u>wināh-i ō puhl šawēd</u>. <u>Wināh-i hamēmālān</u> is
    the sin in which there is a complaint in this world and pay-
    ment as a fine for the sin should be made to that complainer.

Answer 42

.   If there is nothing else implied in this [question],
a Zoroastrian who copulates with a Moslem woman and
owing to this copulation she becomes pregnant, [the
fact of] giving a child to a Moslem is immediately [con-
sidered] a tanāpuhl sin.

.   If this child is born or dies in the womb and produces
lochia, whatever sin which is considered in Islam on this
occasion would afflict his soul. Under this category
fall various fornication sins.

.   If that child reaches the age of fifteen and remains a
Moslem, on the account of this [child] remaining a Moslem,
the conceiver is a margarzān.

.   If the woman is married, he [the violator] has to atone
to her husband for this fornication. [Retaliation for]
fornication is nine hundred stīr [as is the retaliation]
for the sin of the hamēmālān.[1]

.   As for the virgin woman. Taking [her] virginity is a
tanāpuhl sin.

.   If she is a Zoroastrian, retaliation of this fornication
should be paid to the husband or the guardian of the
young woman. Atonement of [the taking of] virginity
also should be paid to the husband or the guardian of
the girl.

---

1.   See note 1 to text of this question.

passox <u>42</u>, cont'd.

8.   ēn ēdōn ka.andar ham daštān māh.any mard marzišnīh.ud

abārīg.i čiyōn andar any dar i abar nibišt.pad-š nēst.

Answer 42, cont'd.

8. Further, what [we] recorded in the previous chapter
    regarding copulation during menstruation and other
    [such sins] does not apply to this [chapter].

pursišn 43

1. ān i pursēd.kū xwasrāyēn¹ az ayōkēn pad čē juttar.ud
jud jud wizārišn čē čiyōn.

passox 43

2. xwasrāyēn wizārihēd júd āyōzišn.ud ān bawēd ka mard
duxt ēd i purnāy hast.uš pid pad ān abar dāštan
wināhkār.ud ziyānag.jud az dastwarīh-i pid.sālār ēd
frāz gīrēd.u-š zan bawēd.ān zan xwasrāyēn xwānīhēd.kār
kunišn i-š bawēd sālār.ziyānag-iz nē xwēš xwarišn ud
wistarag az-š stānēd pādixšā.ud pus-ē zāyēd.ō burnāyīh
rasēd.ziyānag sālār ān i-š kunēd.ka pus-ē zāyēd.ō
burnāyīh mad.ziyānag sālārīh andar ān mard.pad pādixšāīh
zanīh ōy be pādixšā bawēd. pus [ud] duxt andar pānzdah
sāl ān pus zāyēnd hamāg pus duxt-i ān pus bawēnd.ān pus
pusarīh-i kas nēst.

---

1. See A. Perikhanian, "On Some Pahlavi Legal Terms", W.B. Henning
Mem. Vol. (London, 1970), pp. 349-51, also R.HF. pp. 196,198,200.

Question 43

1. This [question he] asked, "What is the differ-
    ence between ayōkēn [wife] and xwasrāyēn [wife]. What
    are the particularities of each [case]?"

Answer 43

2. Xwasrāyēn is different from ayōkēn[-ship]. The case
    [of xwasrāyēn] is this; when a father has a mature
    daughter, the fact of keeping her [unmarried] is sin-
    ful on father's [part], and if the girl without her
    father's approval takes a master [husband], in that
    case she is called a xwasrāy. The master becomes her
    warden. [But] even if this young woman does not take
    [receive] food and clothing [from her husband] it would
    be lawful. [Assume] she gives birth to a son. That boy
    reaches maturity, and [then] the boy becomes responsi-
    ble for the woman [his mother]. If she gives birth to
    [another] son and he reaches maturity the woman [mother]
    under responsibility to that man [her eldest son] be-
    comes his [her husband's] pādixšā wife legally. [If
    any] boy or girl within that fifteen years of the [el-
    dest] son be born, they are considered as the daughter and
    son of the [first] son. That son [the first] cannot
    become an adopted son to anybody.

pursišn 44

1. ayōkēn kadār bawēd.

passox

2. ayōkēn ān bawēd.ka mard-ē be widarān bawēd.uš zan
frazand pādixšāihā ud pus padīraftag.bē duxt-ē kē-š
šōy nē kard ēstēd.ēg-š nēst.u-š stūr-i kardag ud brād-i
hambāy nēst.ān duxt ayōkēn pid ōwōn bawēd čiyōn ka
pādixšā zan-i pid hē.

3. kas pad pādixšāihā zanīh griftan ud dāštan nē pādixšā.
pus ud duxt i-š az-š zāyēnd pādixšāihā frazand-i pidar
hēnd.

Question 44

1. Who is an ayōkēn?

Answer

2. Ayōkēn is a girl who when a man has passed away and
    had had no main wife or children or an adopted son or
    an appointed proxy or a partner brother except a girl
    who is unmarried, then this girl becomes her father's
    ayōkēn with the same privileges as though she had been
    the main wife of her father.

3. No one is legally permitted to take and keep her as main
    wife. Sons and daughters to whom she gives birth are
    legally the children of the father [her father].

Plate of

Comparative Readings of <u>ANK</u>., As Well As

Mine and That Which Is in the MS.

Question and Answer References	BTE. Pages		Folio Nos.
Ans. 1	4	. . اا۱۵۹۶ص۱	123 Verso
Ans. 3	7	. . لس	124 Verso
Ans. 3	7	. . سوما۱۱ص	124 Verso
Ans. 4	11	. . للسایل	125 Verso
Ans. 5	17	. سلا۱۱۹۶ص	127 Recto
Ans. 5	22	. . ۱۶۹۹	128 Verso
Ques. 7	24	اا۱۶۹۹ل . . .	129 Recto
Ques. 9	32	۱۶۹ال۹۱اا ۱۶۹۹سب .	131 Recto
Ans. 9	32	. ۱۶۹۹سسب	131 Recto
Ans. 10	36	لسلا۱۶۹ا ۱۹۵۵سب	132 Recto
Ques. 16	49	. ۱۶۹۹سسبل . .	135 Recto
Ques. 17	53	. ۱۵۶۹۶سل . .	136 Verso
Ques. 17	58	. ۱سوسبل۱۹ا . .	137 Verso
Ques. 17	60	. . سسب .	138 Recto
Ques. 17	62	. . سسبلا	138 Verso
Ques. 19	78	. . ۱۶۹سسواب	143 Recto
Ans. 27	105	. ۱۶۹۹۱ر سب .	150 Recto
Ans. 36	125	۱۶۹سوبلا . .	155 Recto
Ans. 39	137	. ۱سسبسر . .	157 Recto

SOURCES CONSULTED

Pahlavi Texts and Translations

Anklesaria, B. T. The Pahlavi Rivāyat of Ātūr-Farnbag and
Farnbag-Srōs, 2 vols. Bombay, 1969, text with English
transl., edited posthumously by K. M. JamaspAsa.

Anklesaria, T. D., ed. The Dātistān-i Dinik, part I,
pursism I-XL, text, no date.

----------. The Matikān-i Hazār Dātistān, text with intro.
by J. J. Modi, Bombay, 1912.

----------. Rivāyat-i Hēmit-i Ašawahištan, text with
transliteration with intro. by C. Tarapore. Bombay,
1962.

----------. Bundihišn, facsimile ed. of the Ms. TDI, text
with intro. Bonyād-i Fazhang-i Iran. Teheran, 1970.

Asmussen, J. P. xvastvānift, transcription and transl.
Prostant aupd Munksgaard, Copenhagen, 1965.

Bartholomae, C. "Notes on Sarsanian Law," transl. by L.
Bogdanov, with text, transc. and transl. from
Matikān-i Hazār Dātistān. Journal of Cama Oriental
Institute, Bombay, vols. XVIII, 1931, pp. 1-67;
XXVI, 1934, pp. 1-80; XXX, 1963, p. 103; XLI, 1967,
pp. 1-94.

Bulsara, S. J. The Laws of the Ancient Persians as Found
in "Matikān-i Hazar Dātistān," with intro. and
transliteration and transl. of the entire Mh.D.
Bombay, 1937.

Jamasp, D. H., ed. Vendidād. Avestan text with Pahlavi
transl. Bombay, 1907.

JamaspAsa, K. M. "Ēmēt-i Ašavahištān" [transcription and
transl. of passages from BTE.]. Monumentum H. B.
Nyberg, Brill, Leiden, 1975, pp. 435-43.

----------. "Aspects of Kirpak in Zoroastrian Religion"
[transcription and transl. passages from BTE.].
Memorial Jean De Manasce. Louvain, 1974, pp. 237-50.

JamaspAsa, K. M. "Further to Ēmēt-i Ašavahištān" [transc. and transl. passages BTE.]. Munchener Studien zur Sprachwissenschaft. Hft. 30. Munchen, 1972, pp. 65-72.

----------. "On the Ēmēt-i Ašavahištān" [transc. and transl. passages BTE.]. Cama Oriental Institute Golden Jubilee vol. Bombay, 1969, pp. 37-44.

----------. "Eēmēt-i Ašavahištān" [transc. and transl. passages BTE.]. Kuruš mem. vol. Bombay, 1974, pp. 167-79.

JamaspAsana, H. D., ed. Škand Gumānig vičār, Pahlavi-Pazand, with intro. Bombay, 1884.

Madan, M., ed. Dēnkard, text vols. 3, 4, 7, 8. Bombay, 1911.

Marzpān,Faretūn. MS. Rivāyat Hēmit-i Ašawahištan. C. 1620 A.D. Molla Fīrōz Library. Bombay.

Menasce, J. "Problemes des Mazdéens dans l'Iran Musulmān" [transl. passages BTE.]. Festchrift fur Wilhelm Eilers, Otto Harrassowitz. Weisbaden, 1967, pp. 220-30.

----------. "La Rivāyat d'Ēmēt i Ašavahištān" [transl. passages BTE.]. Revue de l'Histoire des Religions. Press Universitaires de France. Paris, 1962, pp. 69-88.

----------. Feux et Fondations pieuses dans le droit Sassanide [with transl. passages BT .]. Paris, 1964.

West, E. W. Šāyast-lā-Šāyast, English transl. SBE. vol. V. Datistān-i Dinik, English transl. SBE. vol. XVIII. Dinkard, Book V, VII, English transl. SBE. vol. XLVII. Dinkard, Book VIII, English transl. SBE. vol. XXXVII. Škand Gumānīk vigar, English trans. SBE. vol. XXIV.

Avestan Texts and Translations

Aši Yašt   Text, ed. K. F. Geldner, Stuttgart, 1886-96.
Text and Persian transl. ed. Pourdawood,
Yašt-hā, Bombay, 1927.
Transcription and notes, ed. Richelt, Avesta
Reader, Berlin, 1968.
Translation, Darmester, SBE. rep. Motilal
Banarsidass, Delhi, 1965.

Ardvisūr Yašt   Text, ed. K. F. Geldner, Stuttgart, 1886-96.
Transcription and notes, ed. Richelt,
Avesta Reader, Berlin, 1968.

Hōm Yašt   Text, ed. K. F. Geldner, Stuttgart, 1886-96.
Transcription and notes, ed. Richelt, Avesta
Reader, Berlin, 1968.
J. M. Unvala, Neryosangh's Sanskrit version
of Hōm Yašt with text transc. transl.
commentary and glossary, Bombay, 1924.

Mihr Yašt   Text, ed. K. F. Geldner.
Transcription and translation, Gershevitch,
Hymn to Mithra, Cambridge, 1959.

Rašn Yašt   Text, ed. K. F. Geldner.
Text and transl. ed. Pourdawood, Yašt-hā,
Bombay, 1927.
Transl. Darmester, SBE. rep. Motilal
Banarsidass, Delhi, 1965.

Srōš Yašt   Text, ed. K. F. Geldner.
Text and transl. ed. Pourdawood, Yašt-hā,
Bombay, 1927.
Translation, Darmester, SBE. rep. Motilal
Banarsidass, Delhi, 1965.

Yasna, nos.   Text with Persian transl., ed. Pourdawood.
30, 31, 45   Transcription and translation, S. Insler,
The Gathas of Zarathushtra, Brill, Leiden,
1975.
M. W. Smith, Studies in Gathic Syntax,
Kraus Reprint Corp., New York, 1966.

Vendidād   Transl., J. Darmester, SBE. vol. IV.
Avestan text and Pahlavi transl., ed.
D. H. Jamasp, Bombay, 1907.

Old Persian (Inscriptions)

Kent, R. G. Old Persian Grammar, text with English transl.
American Oriental Society. New Haven, Conn., 1953.

Sharp, R. N. Farmānhāy-i šāhanšāhān-i Haxāmanišy, text,
Persian transliteration and transl. Pahlavi University
Press. Shirāz, 1965.

Related Subjects

Asmussen, J. P. Manichean Literature: Representative Texts
Chiefly from Middle Persian and Parthians. Delmar.
New York, 1975.

Baily, H. W. The Persian Language, ed. A. Arbery, Legacy
of Persia. Clarendon. Oxford, 1953.

Bartholomae, C. "Woman in Sasanian Law," transl. L. Bogdanov. Bulletin of Iran League. Bombay, 1929.

Bernard, F. The First Year of Roman Law. Oxford University
Press. New York, 1906.

Boyce, M. "Middle Persian Literature," Handbuch der
Orientalistik, 1968.

----------. Letter of Tansar. UNESCO Pub., 1968.

Browne, E. G. A Literary History of Persia, 4 vols.
Cambridge University Press, 1969.

Brunner, C. The Middle Persian Inscription of the Priest
Kirdēr at nags-i Rustann. Near Eastern Numismatic,
Iconography and History Studies, ed. D. Kouymjian, 1974.

----------. Middle Persian Syntax. Delmar. New York, 1977.

Christensen, A. L'Empire des Sassanid. Kobenhaven, 1907.

----------. Le regne du Roi Kawādh et le communism
Mazdakite. Kobenhaven, 1925.

Colledge, A. R. The Parthians. Thames & Hudson. London,
1967.

Desai, S. F. "Some Ancient Societal Laws." Kuruš Mem. vol.
Iran Culture House. Bombay, 1974.

Dhabhar, B. N. <u>Persian Rivāyats of Hormazyār Framarz and Others</u>. English transl. with adapted text and translation of Dd. and Saddar Bundihisn. Cama Oriental Institute. Bombay, 1932.

Dhala, H. "Women in Ancient Iran and India." <u>Kuruš Mem. vol.</u> Iran Culture House. Bombay, 1974, pp. 37-50.

Driver, G. R. <u>Aramaic Documents of the 5th Century</u>. Clarendon. London, 1954.

Duchesne-Guillemin, J. <u>La religion de l'Iran ancien.</u>, transl. K. M. JamaspAsa. Tata Press. Bombay, 1973.

Frye, R. <u>The Heritage of Persia</u>. Weidenfeld and Nicolson. London, 1965.

Gershevitch, I. "Iranian Literature." <u>Literature of the East</u>. Grove Press. New York, 1959.

Ghilain, A. <u>Essai sur la langue Parth</u>. Institut Orientaliste. Louvin, 1939.

Harlez, C. <u>Manuel de la langue Pehlevie</u>. Paris, 1880.

Henning, W. B. "An Astronomical Chapter of Bundihišn." <u>JRAS</u>. London, 1942.

Hastings Kelke, W. H. <u>An Epitom of Roman Law</u>. Sweet and Maxwell Ltd. London, 1901.

Jamaspji, D. H. <u>Ardavirāf nāmeh</u>, revised Pahlavi text with M. Haug's transl. 1872.

Junker, F. J. "The origin of the Avestan Alphabet." <u>Modi Mem. vol.</u> Bombay, 1930, pp. 766-74.

Lord MacKenzie. <u>Studies in Roman Law</u>, 5th ed., rev. W. Blackwood & Sons. London, 1880.

Mirza, H. K. "Sogdian Plural Suffix in Pahlavi." 26th <u>International Congress of Orientalists</u>, vol. II, 1968.

----------. <u>Outline of Parsi History</u>. Bombay, 1974.

Modi, J. J. "The Evolution of Iranian Law." <u>Jackson Mem. vol.</u> Bombay, 1954.

Modi, J. J. "The Mobadān Mobad Omid bin Ashavst. Referred to by Hamza Isphahāni." Studia Indo Iranica. Liepzig, 1931, pp. 274-88.

----------. The Religious Ceremonies and Customs of the Parsees. Bombay, 1922.

Mojtaba, Minovi, ed. Nāmeh-i Tansar. Kharazmie Pub. Teheran, 1975.

Molé, M. "Le problem Zurvanite." Journal Asiatique, 1959, vol. 247, pp. 431-69.

Muirhead, J. Historical Introduction to the Private Law of Rome. Adam & Charles Black. Edinburgh, 1886.

Perikhanian, A. "On Some Pahlavi Legal Terms." W. B. Hennings Mem. vol. Lund Humpheries. London, 1970, pp. 349-57.

Salemann, C. A Middle Persian Grammar, transl. L. Bogdanov. British India Press. Bombay, 1930.

Sykes, P. A History of Persia, 2 vols. Macmillan. London, 1963.

Unvala, J. M. Observations on the Religion of the Parthians. Bombay, 1925.

Widengren, G. Mani and Manichaeism. Weidenfeld and Nicolson. London, 1965.

Zaehner, R. C. Zurvan: A Zoroastrian Dilemma. Biblo and Tannen. New York, 1972.

----------. The Dawn and the Twilight of Zoroastrianism. Weidenfeld and Nicolson. London, 1961.

----------. Teaching of the Magi. Oxford University Press. London, 1955.

Dictionaries

Abrahamian. Pahlavi Dictionary, with English, Russian, Armenian and Persian transl. Yerevān, 1965.

Bahar, M. Bundihišn Glossary. Bonyād-i Farhang-i Iran. Teheran, 1967.

----------. Vičitakihā-i Zādspram Glossary. Bonyād-i Farhang-i Iran. Teheran, 1973.

Bartholomae, C. Altiranisches Worterbuch. Berlin, 1961.

Dhabhar, B. N., ed. Pahlavi Yasna Visperad, with glossary and intro. Bombay, 1949.

Faravashi, B. Farhang-i Pahlavi, 2nd ed. Teheran University Press. Teheran, 1974.

Junker, F. J. Farhang-i Pahlavik, ed. and intro. Heidlberg, 1912.

----------. Farhang-i Pahlavik, in Zeichengemässer Anordung Otto Harrassovitz. Leipzig, 1955.

Kapadia, D. Glossary of Pahlavi Vendidād. Poona, 1953.

MacKenzie, D. N. A Concise Pahlavi Dictionary. Oxford University Press. London, 1971.

Mashkūr, M. J. Farhang-i huzvarišhāyi Pahlavi. Bonyād-i Farhang-i Iran. Teheran, 1968.

Nyberg, H. S. A Manual of Pahlavi, 2 vols. Otto Harrasso-vitz. Weisbaden, 1964.

Tafazzoli, A. Glossary of Mēnōg-i xrad. Bonyad-i Farhang-i Iran. Teheran, 1969.

SELECT GLOSSARY

OF

SOME RELIGIO - LEGAL TERMS

     The following terms are of great significance in Zoroastrian religion. Those with the following numbers refer to their occurrences in this work. Those without number are just to show their significance in Zoroastrian religion even though they have not been mentioned in this text in particular.

<u>A</u>

ahlawdād: A stipend either in cash or kind given by people to the
priest to support him financially so that he can perform
religious ceremonies and duties without being obliged
to do other jobs to support his family.

Q.7.26   PP. 46, 183

akdēn: A non Zoroastrian, generally applied to a Zoroastrian
convert to Islam.

Q.1.4.19.   PP. 3, 19, 141

ans. 4.19   PP. 21, 145

Amahraspand: (Av. amaša spənta) Holy immortals who preside over
spiritual qualities as well as over material creations.

ans. 17.   P. 111

Aša: The concept of truth in Zoroastrianism is not only
verbal or ethical principle but cosmic order as well.
Aša implies truth, righteousness, holiness, order.

Ātaš: Fire, Av. ātar. In the Zoroastrian religion fire is
especially venerated as the shining emblem of Ahura
Mazdā. In the avesta ātar is addressed as the deity
full of glory and full of healing remedies (Ny.5-6).
It is called Master of the House (Y.17-11). It is
called the son of Ahura Mazdā (Y.25-7, 71-10), it is

the representative of Ahura Mazdā . The presence of
Fire in all Zoroastrian ceremonies is inevitable.
The Fire is venerated, prayers are offered unto the
Fire, and the devotee longs to approach Ahura Mazdā
through the Fire.

Five Kinds of Fire

According to the Avesta (Y.17-11) there are five kinds
of visible and invisible fires as the following:

1. Ātar berzi-savah, Pah. ātaš-i buland sūd
The Fire highly beneficient. It is the fire that takes
food only and no water. It is the burning fire in
Ātaš-i Bahrām. Ātaš-i Bahrām is the Fire which should
be established where ever Zoroastrians abide. It is
believed that without the assistance and power of Ātaš-i
Bahrām not a single Zoroastrian could have lived in the
world. For the establishment of this Fire 1001 Fires
should be collected according to strict religious rites
and observations.

2. Ātar vohu-fryāna, Pah. ātaš-i weh franaftār, the
Fire diffusing goodness. This Fire is in the body of
men and animals. This Fire drinks water and takes food.

3. Ātar urvāzišta, Pah. ātaš-i frāx ziwišn, the Fire
of prosperous life. This Fire is in vegetation and
takes water only, no food.

4. Ātar vāzišta, Pah. ātaš-i vāzišt, the Fire that
is the swiftest. The Fire that is in clouds, in atmosphere,

in the earth, in the moutains. This Fire needs no
food and no water.

5. Ātar spiniŝta, Pah. ātaŝ-i abzōnīg, the bountiful
Fire. It is the burning Fire in spiritual state in
the highest heaven before **Ohrmazd**.

The above description of the Fires slightly differs from
that given in Bundahiŝn, in which the fire burning before
Ohrmazd is ātaŝ-i Bahrām. Otherwise both texts concur.
(adaptation from OPH).

As for the sacred Fire Temple foundations; there are
five which are the most revered ones: Ātaŝ-i Bahrām,
Ātaŝ-i burzēn Mehr, Ataŝ-i Adarān, Ātaŝ-iGuŝnasp,
Ataŝ-i Farnbag.

Ātaŝ-i Bahrām: For the establishment of which 1001 fires should be
collected. Wherever the Zoroastrians live it is necessary
to establish Ātaŝ-i Bahrām. No other person except
dastūrs and hērbeds are allowed to look at it.
(R.HF. pp. 62-72)

Ātaŝ-i Burzēn Mehr: Is believed to be the fire that Zoroaster
brought with the censer from the Court of Ohrmazd.
(R.HF. p. 72)

Ātaš-i Adarān: In every quarter where ten Zoroastrian families

live, this Fire should be established with an attendant

engaged on a salary. Once every year this Fire should

be collected and taken to the side of the Bahram Fire

so that the former may be extinguished in front of the

latter.

Ātaš-i Gušnasp: A Sasanian Fire Temple, the remains of which is in

Takht-i Suleymān Azarbāyijān (Iran). This is the only

one in any Fire Temple, ancient or modern, where a

sacred fire is burnt in what is essentially a corridor-

room, where pilgrims could approach the sacred Fire like

servitors coming into the presence of a king, instead

of merely passing by from one doorway to the next,

while the Fire itself is guarded from any danger of

pollution. (Adapted from, M. Boyce, "On the Zoroastrian

Temple Cult of Fire" JAOS, 1975, p. 465.

Ātaš-i Farnbag: whose foundations together with Ātaš-i burzēn Mehr

and Ātas-i Gušnasp, by Sassanian times was lost in the

mists of legend and was associated with the origin of

the world. M. Boyce, op. cit. p. 459.

THE FIRE AS THE DIVINE JUDGE

The Fire deity presides over the red blazing fire, and

acts as divine judge at the final judgment. The Fire as the divine

judge appears variously in the Avesta and justice will be administered through heat, fire, in various form: metal, molten metal, shining

metal. Y.31-3, 34-4, 36-2, 47-6, 31-19, 51-9, 43-4, 30-7, 32-7,

51-9, 31-3, (Adaptation from OPH).

āyōken: A girl whose father or brother have passed away and they

have had no main wife or children by their main wife nor

had they an adopted son or an appointed proxy, then she

becomes ayōkēn of her father or brother. That is she

becomes privileged as though she had been the main wife

of her father or brother. No one is legally permitted

to take her as main wife. Sons or daughters to whom

she gives birth are legally the children of the deceased

father or brother.

Q.1.2.31.44   PP. 3, 11, 207, 289

ans. 1.2.18.23.43.44   PP. 5, 11, 137, 161, 163, 169,

171, 287, 289

ayōkēn Stūr: A girl who under the above mentioned conditions becomes

the family proxy.

Q.1.2   PP. 3.11

ans. 1   P. 5

B

barsnum: A ritual. Ceremonial ablution which should be taken under

the supervision of the **master** of purification rite. It

is a lengthy procedure comprising 21 times washing of

the body with cattle urine and drying it with dust and

again washing with pure water, while at each stage certain

prayers are recited by the master of the purification

as well as by the polluted person. Thereafter a retreat
of nine nights should be observed. After the lapse of
three nights the participant should wash his or her head
and body with cattle urine and water under restrict rules
and regulation and under the supervision of an authority.

ans. 13.34.37   PP. 80, 230, 238

bayaspān: A term designating a girl or a woman who takes a husband
out of her own choice without consultation or approval of
her parents or authorities. According to A. Perikhanian
this word is another version of xwasrāy marriage which
denotes the same conception.

ans. 31   P. 211

baxt: Destiny, a conception which is not much favored by Zoroastrians, since according to their religious ethics it is
the will power of every individual which determines his
or her life, **Ohrmazd** never dooms or favors anyone in
advance.

Q. and ans. 40   PP. 265, 269

C

Činwad Puhl: The divider bridge which separates the soul of the
righteous   ones   who cross, from those of the wicked
ones who fall off into hell.

ans. 39   P. 249

čagar wife: (lit. collateral wife) If a woman is married and her
              husband dies, if she remarries then her marital status
              is of an inferior one to that of the main wife. That
              is she has not full authority over her children. Her
              husband is not fully responsible for her food and clothing.
              She belongs to her former husband who has a share in
              her children by her second husband.

              Q. 7-23-31   PP. 46, 159, 207

              ans. 1.7.23.31   PP. 7, 52, 171, 209

<u>D</u>

drahm: A silver coin almost in value about 2 pence sterling.

              Q. 18   P. 127

              ans. 18.23   PP. 131, 173

drūg: The principle of lie, evil which brings disorder and
              chaos as against <u>Aša</u>. (see p. 300)

dastšōy: A cult term designating the ceremony of ablution with
              cattle urine and consecrated water.

              Q. 14.33   PP. 82, 219

              ans. 33.37   PP. 221, 237

daštān nišastan: Menstruation enclosure. If a woman is in menses
      or
daštānestan: a place should be prepared for her, thirty steps away
              from barsam (holy twigs), thirty steps away from sacred
              place, and three steps away from pious man. She should
              not talk with any pious man, should not gaze at fire,

should not look at the sun. Food should be carried to her in metallic utensils **in company** with a bowl of cattle urine and a bowl of pure water **and special** linen gloves. Before starting to eat she should wash her hands and face three times with cattle urine, three times with water and should put on the gloves and take up her food in such a way that the hands may not come in contact with the food. This seclusion should last for nine nights (adap. R.HF).

ans. 33   P. 221

dūdag kadag bānūg: The first lady of the family. A status which gives full independence to the woman regarding her family affairs.

Q. 3   P. 13

ans. 5   P. 37

dūdag sālār: A term including:

-- status as head of the family.

-- the power to make decisions for and in the name of the absent paterfamilias analogous to the powers of an executor.

Q. 5   P. 25

ans. 5   P. 27

dwāzdah-homāst: A religious ceremony performed in honor or in memory of a woman either living or dead.

ans. 17   P. 111

F

frasgird (fraškard): The ultimate renovation when evil shall be
delivered in the two hands of the Truth. (Y.30-8., 48-2)
This concept is repeatedly referred to in Avesta. A
few are the following: Y.30-9, Y.34-15, Y.55-6, Yt. 19-89
(adap. OPH).

ans. 31   P. 209

G

gadar: A term used to designate a lover, an unofficial husband.

ans. 5.42   PP. 37, 42, 43, 283

gahanbar: Av. yāirya (annual, yearly), season festivals. There are
six gāhānbārs in a year and each of them is celebrated
for five days.

1. maidyōzarem (mid-spring)

2. maidyōshahem (mid-summer)

3. **paitishahem** (harvest-time)

4. **ayāthrem** (approaching of winter)

5. **maidyārem** (mid-winter)

6. hamaspathmaedem (equinox)

(adapt. OPH).

ans. 17   P. 111

Ganāg-Mēnōg: Av. Angra-mainyū, the destructive power of the world
(evil). In Pahlavi literature it is identified as Ahreman.

ans. 12   P. 75

garōdmān: The highest section of heaven.

ans. 39   P. 249

gomēz: Cattle urine used for washing as preliminary steps for
ablutions and ceremonial purifications.

Q. 14   P. 82

ans. 34   P. 227

<u>H</u>

hamēmālān wināh: There are three kinds of sins: wināh-i ruwānīg
(lit. a sin which afflicts the soul), wināh-i ō puhl sāwēd
(lit. a sin which determines the passage over the bridge
in the final day), wināh-i hamēmālān which is a sin in
which there is a complaint in this world and payment as
a fine for the sin should be made to that complainer.
For the other two categories of the sins there are also
series of atonements the performance of which will wash
off the sin except certain cases which only death is
the atonement.

ans. 42   P. 283

Hammistagān: Neutral station between heaven and hell.

ans. 26.39   PP. 187, 261

hamrēd: Av. ham raēΘwa, direct defilement.

Q. 15   P. 86

hāθra: A unit of measure which has three variations:

          -- hāθra-i meh (great hāθra), 12,000 feet.

          -- hāθra-i keh (small hāθra), 6 to 8,000 feet.

          -- hāθra-i mayānag (middle hāθra), 10,000 feet.

          Q. 13   P. 78

          ans. 13   P. 80

hērbed: A teacher priest.

          Q. 9.11.12.14   PP. 56, 64, 68, 70, 82

          ans. 10   P. 62

hixr: Bodily refuse, including bones, flesh, skin, blood, pus,

          hair, nails, semen, genital discharges and sweat.

          Q. 16   P. 88

humat: good thoughts

hūxt: good words   the maxim of Zoroastrian religion and laws.

huwaršt: good deeds

J

jeh: A whore.

          Appendix ans. 5.   ans. 12   pp. 42, 43, 76

jizyeh: A poll tax levied on non-Moslems when Iran fell in Arabs.

K

kadag-xwadāy: A similar position as dūdag sālār. See p. 307.

          ans. 3.5   PP. 15,33

Khub: Is a stage of proficiency for performing religous cere-
          monies. It needs especial training. There are two
          kinds of Khubs: greater and smaller. A priest who has
          reached the stages of the greater Khub is qualified to
          perform higher liturgical services.

          ans. 14   P. 85

M

margarzān: A sin for which there is no atonement and death is the
            punishment for it.

            ans. 1.4.5.10.11.31.42   PP. 7,21,35,62,66,209,283

Mihrigān: "The festival of the sun," on the 16th day of the 7th
           month (21st day of March, the first Zoroastrian month
           begins), this festival is held. There is a legendary
           history connected with this event. It is believed that
           the first legendary king Ferēydūn imprisoned Zohāk
           (symbol of evil ruling force) and ascended the throne
           of Iran on this day.

           See norūz for 21st of March.

mowbedān mowbēd: The supreme spiritual master whose authority was
                  parallel to that of the king.

                  Several terms are used to designate religious status of
                  a Zoroastrian. Although the original significance is
                  lost, the following terms are used in general parlour
                  for religous titles and in religious ceremonies.

-- Āsrō, a priest, a member of priestly class.

-- Behdēn, a Zoroastrian, a member of Zoroastrian laity.

-- Khurd, minor, small. This is applied to a child
(male or female) of Zoroastrian parents before the
child is duly admitted into the Zoroastrian religion
by performing Navjot ceremony. Generally this ceremony is performed after a child completes seven years
and before attaining puberty.

-- Hāvišt, a religious disciple, a candidate for priesthood.

-- Hērbed, a teacher priest.

-- Mowbed, an officiating priest.

-- Dastūr (dastwar), a chief priest, an authorized head
of the priests belonging to a particular Fire Temple
or congregation. (adapt. from OPH.)

N

nog nāwar: A ceremony for initiating a candidate in priesthood.

ans. 17   P. 111

nōruz: New year (21st of March). It is believed that the legendary
king Jamšid of pēšdādiyān dynasty first observed it. The
Sassanian kings had a public audience on this day. There
are controvertial views on the exact equivalent of nōrūz
in Gregorian Calendar.

P

pādixsā wife: Main wife, a wife who is independent with full authority
regarding her children. Her husband is fully responsible

for providing her food, clothing and other expenses.

She can become family guardian after her husband's death.

Q. 1.7   PP. 3, 46

ans. 1.2.7.18.31.43   PP 5, 11, 48, 139, 211, 287

padrēd: Av. Paiti-raēϴwa, indirect defilement.

Q. 15   P. 86

pad pēšag šustan: one of the meanings of pēšag is a knot in a stick
and it implies as a part for the whole, the particular
name of a religious ceremony of washing or purification
after pollution, more especially after contact with a
dead body. The chief implement in this purificatory
ablution is a pišak (pēšeg), a stick of nine knotes to
which a ladle of lead or iron is attached to pour out
gōmēz (sanctified urine of a bull) on the contaminated
person. The idiom pad pēšāg šustan refers to this
Baršnūm ablution. D. Kapadia, Glossary of Vendidād
(Bombay, 1953), p. 46.

ans. 19.32   PP. 145, 217

paoiryāi dāmanan: An Avestic term denoting the first created beings.
In this text and according to Hēmīt's explanation it
refers to primitive uncivilized men who follow the law
of nature in that whoever first seizes a thing owns it.

ans. 4.25.   PP. 21, 181

petīt pad gowišn: verbal repentance. The question of penance is of

great significance in Zoroastrianism. If a Zoroastrian

commits a crime either verbally or physically she should

be made to repent of it. The ordering of the retribution

should be made by a dastūr and in proportion to the crime.

If ordered in excess of the sin, the dastūr becomes a

sinner. A penitential formula is to be recited daily.

If a person can not recite it then he should assign another

person to perform it for him. The most cardinal peni-

tential formula which is necessary to be recited daily

is the following:

"I am sorry for and repentant and in renunciation of

every sin which I have spoken, which I have done, which

has arisen through me and which I have imagined."

Q. 39   P. 243

R

ristāxēz: Resurrection of the dead.

ans. 39   P. 259

Rivāyat: The word Rivāyat does not occur in **Pahlavi** texts. It appears

that the word Rivāyat was applied to certain **Pahlavi**

writings at a later date. Also the word seems to be a

Persian-Arabic hybrid word, a combination of Pahlavi rawāg,

Persian ravā (current, what is practiced) and Arabic **riwāya**

(report, account).

The word is used to designate a certain type of literature both in **Pahlavi** and Persian language. These **literatures** comprise explanations of religious rules and regulations in question-dialogue form always posed to and answered by a high priest.

rūspi: A courtesan

          Appendix ans. 5   PP. 42, 43

S

sih-gām: "Thirty steps": The minimum distance allowed for any polluted thing to be near the fire, water, and barsam (the holy twigs used in liturgical ceremonies).

          ans. 14   P. 84

sinag masāy ⎫
bāzā masāy ⎬   Av. bāzu stavaghem vā sraoni masanghem: a free translation of which would be "as much as can be sufficient to make both ends meet."

          Q. 23   P. 159

          ans. 5.18   PP. 33, 133

Sošyāns: The saviour who will bring about the ultimate Renovation and eternal bliss.

          ans. 39   P. 251

Spēnāg Mēnōg: Av. spanta mainyū, Bountious spirits, the creative power of the world. In later Avesta and Pahlavi literature spenāg-mēnōg and **Ohrmazd** became the same entity.

          ans. 12.17   PP. 75, 110

spihr: Celestial governing sphere, firmament, fate, sky. In

            certain religious beliefs it is believed that spihr governs

            men's destiny. An idea which is totally rejected by an

            orthodox Zoroastrian. In Zoroastrianism, free will

            determines man's life.

            Q. 40   P. 265

stīr: A weight of 6 1/2 drahm. Each drahm is a silver coin of

            about 2 pence sterling in value.

            ans. 3.12.18-41   PP. 15, 74, 131, 277

stōš: The fourth morning after death when it is believed that

            the judgment of the man's deed takes place. Therefore

            imploring God's blessings and mercy by the relatives and

            friends of the deceased on this particular occasion is

            considered a benefaction.

            ans. 26.29.39.   PP. 185, 199, 251

stūr: A legal term with a wide range of applications such as

            proxy, guardian, adopted son (who ultimately would function

            as a proxy), and curator.

            Q. 1.18   PP. 3, 127

            ans. 1.2.23   PP. 5, 11, 169, 171

stūr-i būdag: When a paterfamilias passes away, his son who is sane

            and has reached the age of 15 is chosen as the family proxy.

            (There is no sharp distinction between stūr and dūdag salār.

The three terms būdag, kardag and gūmardag apply to
both. See p. 6.)
ans. 5   P. 27

stūr-i kardag: A proxy who is assigned according to the religious
law directly by and in the lifetime of the paterfamilias.
The eligibility for this assignment is to be a mentally
sound male member of the family, of 15 years of age.
ans 1   P. 5

stūr-i gumārdag: After passing away of a paterfamilias, he who is
most eligible will be chosen as a family proxy by the
authorities of the time.
ans. 1   P. 5

T

taïg: A term relating to a precautional extra day allowed
before a woman can take final ablution after each menstruation.
Q. 33   P. 219
ans. 33   P. 221

tanapuhl: A sin which disables the sinner from passing the činwad
bridge. The atonement for it is 300 stīrs.
ans. 1.4.5.7.21.25.31.41.42   PP. 7, 21, 35, 48, 151,
181, 209, 277, 283

tan-i pasēn: The ultimate form of existence that will be given to the
Universe after the current cycle has elapsed.

Q. 39   P. 245

ans. 39   P. 261

tan rēman: A religious ceremony for an especial ablution for the purification of body and soul. There are four types of purification according to the degree of the body or soul pollution: **pādyāb**, nāhm, tan-rēman and baršnūm.

ans. 37   P. 237

W

weh dēn: "The good religion." Zoroastrian religion as usually
referred to by Zoroastrians.

Q. 1.19   PP. 3, 141

ans. 38   PP. 241, see note 1, P. 242.

X

Xādrāy/**xwāsrāy** wife: A girl who marries a man without the consent or
approval of her parents or authorities. In this case the
man becomes her warden but is not obliged to provide all
her expenses. If she gives birth to a son when he reaches
the age of 15 then she becomes Padixšā wife of her husband.

Q. 43   P. 287

ans. 43   P. 287

xšvaš manghō (av.): "six months process." If a woven cloth becomes
        polluted, it should be washed six times by cattle urine,
        six times rubbed with dust, six times washed by pure
        water and afterwards it shall be exposed to the air for
        six months through the window of the house.
        ans. 16   P. 90

xwēdōdāh: Next of kin marriage. A practice advocated in Zoroastrian
        religion entailing many benefactions. But it seems that
        not only it is not practiced amongst the later Zoroastrian
        generation, the idea is totally rejected.
        Q. 22.27.28.29.30   PP. 155, 189, 193, 197, 203
        ans. 17.22.27.28.29.30   PP. 111, 157, 191, 195, 199, 205

<u>Y</u>

Yašts: A series of prayers each dedicated to an specific deity.
        The word **yaštan** which is the infinitive of the same word
        has a wide range of applications such as to offer prayer,
        to worship, to consecrate, to recite religious incantations.
        ans. 14   P. 84

Yašt-i wirāst: A religious ceremony performed by priests for qualifying
        themselves for the greater <u>Khub</u> in order to be able to
        perform higher liturgical rites.
        ans. 14   P. 84

yoždahrgar: Master of the ceremonial purification rites.
        Q. 10   P. 60
        ans. 12   P. 72

Z

zamānag: A term designating a period of time (one year) during
which a proxy must be assigned for a family whose paterfamilias has passed away.

ans. 3   P. 15

ziyānag: Initially it means a young women, but in legal term as
Bartholomae has defined it, denotes collateral wife.

ans. 7.23   PP. 48, 161

This is a Revised Edition of the original dissertation
which is available in the Columbia University Libraries